Profit: The Stupid View
of President Donald Trump

Philip McShane

M.Sc., Lic. Phil., S.T.L., D. Phil. Oxon.

AXIAL PUBLISHING
Vancouver

Axial Publishing
www.axialpublishing.com

Canadian Cataloguing in Publication Data
McShane, Philip, 1932 –
Profit: The Stupid View of President Donald Trump
ISBN   978-1-988457-01-7
1. Economics   2. Human Science   I. Title

Text layout and cover:
James Duffy
Patrick Brown
Alberto Luna Martínez

To my Wife,

Reverend Sally,

who searches with me

for the phoenix that is to rise

out of the negative beginning of the Anthropocene Age

Contents

PREFACE

Do I not have your attention? But the title is, alas, more than attention-getting: it is brutally and destructively true of Trump. Of course, the stupid view is shared by Donald's minions: that boosts the destructiveness, or at least perpetuates the present moral mess. And then there are the Koch brothers,[1] helping stupidity, and its twin cupidity, to preserve the haughty abuse of the middle and lower classes.[2] And there are legions of other money-spinners that haunt our dollars and our dreams.[3]

How might I help you to identify the stupidity, the haughtiness, the abuse? Think, perhaps, of election or government promises regarding wages or general increasing of middleclass purchasing power. A quiet but serious

---

[1] Jane Mayer, *Dark Money: The Hidden History of the Billionaires Behind the Rise of the Radical Right* (New York: Doubleday, 2016), tells their story. We shall muse on their shenanigans later in various ways, but I note here a point re their operations during the Obama years, when "they said they were driven by principle, but their positions dovetailed seamlessly with their personal financial interests." *Dark Money*, 4. Did they suffer financially during those years? "Despite their predictions that Obama would prove catastrophic to the American economy, Charles and David's personal fortunes had nearly tripled during his presidency, from $14 billion apiece in March 2009 to $41.6 billion each in March, 2015. *Ibid.*, 377–78. For a sniff of their sick power there is the documentary film (2014) by Carl Deal and Tia Lessin, *Citizens Koch*.

[2] The haughtiness has many shades. I think of Bernard Lonergan's remark about deep flaws in economic theory and practice: "the long overdue basic expansion is doled out to one's fellow countrymen under the haughty name of welfare." *Macroeconomic Dynamics: An Essay in Circulation Analysis*, ed. Frederick Lawrence, et al., vol. 15, *Collected Works of Bernard Lonergan* (Toronto: University of Toronto Press, 1999, 86. The haughtiness prevails in the various brands of socialism and pseudo-democracy. The haughtiness lurks in Obama's recent claim, "The profit motive can be a powerful force for the common good, driving businesses ..." "The Way Ahead," *The Economist*, October 8, 2016, 22–26. Such is the stupid view of the outgoing president: but that is a story to be discovered, a massive critical sublation of the story told in Suskind's book on Obama's education, referenced in note 17 below.

[3] There is a general documentary film from Autumn 2016 that would entertain and depress: *Meet the Donors*, directed by Alexandra Pelosi.

i

pause over the non-stupid view of profit exposes the silliness, the abusiveness, the immorality: one does not need the ponderous research of Piketty.[4] Perhaps, indeed, it would be best to begin with a comment on that problem of wages: with a quiet pause, a slow pleasant climb, a dummy dalliance.[5] So: do I not encourage your serious dalliance by making the claim that, with the implementation of a non-stupid view of profit, you would find your wages doubling within six years? So much, then, for the haughty suggestion of, say, a guaranteed annual increase of 3%.[6]

We'll get on with the wake up, and the Anthropocenic waking, of stupidity, through a series of short chapters. The stupid view is best recognized when you have a grip on a correct view. Is XXV + XIIX equal to XXXXVII? Doesn't it look good for equality; don't the sides correspond, 7 to seven? Not if you know the meaning of X and V.

Does the gross national product add up to happiness? It is not beyond our dumminess to know that only some of the product, say a set named X, brightens our lives. A new car? Yes, that is normally a lift in our lives, so a member of the set X. But a new car factory? Perhaps it is a thing of beauty and a joy for the eyes, an aesthetic happiness. But, really, it is only a V-hickle (LOL) for X. The fact that money flows to buy both does not measure my happiness. Do, can, X and V be connected in a non-stupid fashion, so as to ground genuine promises of a president or a parliament, so as to ground happiness?

Well, now, there's a place to start. But let's be honest. If a smart guy like Donald can't figure this out, it may take a little time for us underpaid dummies!

---

[4] Thomas Piketty, *Capital in the Twenty-First Century*, translated by Arthur Goldhammer (Cambridge: Harvard University Press, 2014). Popular media, and indeed some economists, exaggerated the innovative quality of Piketty's work. In fact such work had been ongoing in the U.S. Further, Piketty's main point, that the rich are getting richer, has been common knowledge for some time.
[5] "Dummy", of course, is ambiguous. There is a deep sense in which money is a dummy. This, of course, is not my first shot at this stuff, but my promise here is to dodge side-issues, to bring you to the point step by step. It does require a serious imaginative effort. If you find this too seemingly easy or incomplete, you can venture into my *Piketty's Plight and the Global Future: Economics for Dummies* (Vancouver, BC: Axial Publishing, 2014) or, my more comprehensive book, *Economics for Everyone: Das Just Kapital* (Halifax: Axial Publishing, 1998).
[6] On the scientific key to the massive change, see note 13 of chapter 6 below, p. 35.

I must add a cautionary note. I mention the car as a piece of present happiness. Is it really, and is it thus permanently, hybrid or high-breed? Is military expansion or Obamacare or gun-possession a global joy? These questions reach beyond my question regarding income. Happiness and global joy, quality of life, climate, toy and transport: these are issues that weave into my focus. But my focus is on income, not on the character of its disposal.[7]

At this stage you may well be thinking that it is time I talked some about President Trump's stupidity, and, yes, I can't gloss over it entirely in this little Preface. But the cautionary note of the previous paragraph applies here. The president has, no doubt, some bold ideas and hopes on a range of issues, but on the issue of profit he shares a common muddle. We will get into details of that muddle slowly, but perhaps it is enough in my short Preface to give an obvious identification. I appeal, then, to one whom I consider to be the Grande Dame of 20th century economics, Joan Robinson.[8] In a little book of 1970 she sweeps through the history of the muddling, the core of which I wish to focus on. She has no solution to that muddle, though in the years to follow she pushed neatly in the right direction.[9] But here she is, as she

---

[7] Character? Characters? The direction of economic innovation and deepening is our massive topic. But I would note here, as a nudge towards thinking towards an ethos of sanity, that there are characters, sick folk, out there "who have to be cured of their appetite for making more and more money that they may have more money to invest and so make more money and have more money to invest." Bernard Lonergan, *For a New Political Economy*, ed. Philip McShane, vol. 21, *Collected Works of Bernard Lonergan* (Toronto: University of Toronto Press, 1998), 98. My issue of income paradoxically ties in, not with Keynes on employment, but with leisure, with unemployment. Capital deepening and widening need a far deeper human ethos. "If the deepening is not used for further widening, then it must augment leisure. Such leisure may indeed be wasted, just as anything else can be wasted. But if it is properly employed, then it yields the cultural development that effects a new transformation." *Ibid.*, 22. That transformative shift from the industrious revolution is related to much more than climate change. Finally, I would note the abundant literature on that problem, yet come to recommend here the short cry of Roy Scranton, *Learning to Die in the Anthropocene Age: Reflections on the End of a Civilization* (San Francisco: City Lights Books, 2015). To Scranton's pointing I return later, especially in the final chapter.

[8] There is no problem in googling her achievements. On the negativity of her reception in America see Marjorie Turner, *Joan Robinson and the Americans* (New York: M. E. Sharpe, 1990).

[9] I dealt with her creative efforts in the little book mentioned at the end of note 5 above.

winds to a conclusion in the little book mentioned, talking of a vulgarized view that, yes, the President holds even without proclamation. "The vulgarized economic doctrines that enter into the stream of public opinion still proclaim the beneficial operation of the unimpeded play of the profit motive."[10] Two pages further on she adds a relevant comment on Wicksell's and Marshall's tricky weaving together of self-interest and public duty. "There is an obvious fallacy in this doctrine. If the pursuit of profit is the criterion of proper behavior there is no way of distinguishing between productive activity and robbery."[11] It is sadly amusing to find her then being able to call on Al Capone who spoke of his belief in the American System. "My rackets are run on strictly American lines and they are going to stay that way." [12]   Obviously, I am not accusing the American president of racketeering. But the issue is, are the lines of profiteering going to stay that same way, profiteering lauded as good economics?

Am I not just vamping round here with an old complaint, recently aired in the U.S. by an anti-Wall Street movement, more visibly expressed by objecting crowds round international monetary gatherings? But my vamp is to be not only beguilingly sexy but—yes—to eventually be successful. So, thinking of these objecting crowds, of marches against institutions of finance and government, of daily groanings in town and gown, I am led to give a twist to the first words of Marx's Communist Manifesto, replacing *Europe* with *Economics* and *communism* with *complaint*: "A spectre is haunting Economics—the spectre of complaint. All the powers of the old Economics have entered into a holy alliance to exorcise this spectre: Pope and Tsar, Metternich and Guizot, French radicals and German policemen." I could list names of contemporary members of this alliance, and you certainly could fill it out from your local politico-economic situation. But, rather than such listing representative of a complex of situations, I home in strategically on one situation—the Oval office—and on one influential person's stupid clinging to the Old Economics. [13] Those familiar with my work on

---

[10] Joan Robinson, *Freedom and Necessity: An Introduction to the Study of Society* (London: Allen and Unwin, 1970), 114.

[11] *Ibid.*, 116.

[12] *Ibid.*

[13] The Old Economics? The stuff of present texts. A previous effort focused on Gregory Mankiw, whose text *Principles of Economics* is now in its seventh printing and is used worldwide. His work is critiqued in detail in Bruce Anderson and Philip McShane, *Beyond Establishment Economics: No Thank-you Mankiw* (Halifax: Axial Publishing, 2002).

situational-analysis will get the point immediately.[14] My homing in on a precise sickness of the Oval Office is a pointer towards an effective intervention that is part of a futurology, a global cosmopolis of care, that "is concerned to make operative the timely and fruitful ideas that otherwise are inoperative."[15]

An evident problem of my homing in, my focus, is that it will appear to lack context.[16] Should I not have weaved in the story of the White House, or of America's story of finance, including the evolution of Wall Street? I think of such a context as Ron Suskind's *Confidence Men*, which deals with the Obama days, one focus of which was the "banking industry, which over the past couple of decades has grown vast and insatiable by inventing, for the most part, new ways to market, sell, and invest debt."[17] There is early talk, in that book, of Robert Wolf—a regular character in the drama—being "ahead of the curve in grasping the nature and implications of the crisis."[18] Half way through the book there is mention of "a Mensa murderers' row"[19]—Stiglitz, Rogoff, Sachs, Klugman sitting across the table from Summers, Geithner, and Romer, gathered by Obama to view the mess remedially. Later Suskind writes of "the legacy of the behemoth corporations, working in deft coordination, that rose from U.S. soil eventually to span the globe and that lifted small groups of civic-minded men, graced with wealth, who'd gathered to solve the world's intractable problems."[20] Near the end of the book there is a description of a class with about seventy students faced by Alan Kreuger

---

[14] The basic presentation of the dynamics of situational analysis is in chapter sixteen of Philip McShane, *The Allure of the Compelling Genius of History*, Axial Publishing, Vancouver, 2016. A more immediately relevant brief take on it with be given in chapter 12 below. Here and there we return to the Oval office and its possible efforts: see, in particular, below, 70-73, 128-9, 135.

[15] Bernard Lonergan, *Insight: A Study of Human Understanding*, ed. Frederick Crowe and Robert Doran, vol. 3, *Collected Works of Bernard Lonergan* (Toronto: University of Toronto Press, 1992), 264.

[16] I would note that my concluding remarks here are somewhat parallel to Bernard Lonergan's answer to one of three objections he anticipates being made to his view of economic science. "A third objection may take the form that we arrive at an historical synthesis without attempting any historical research." *For a New Political Economy*, 9.

[17] Ron Suskind, *Confidence Men: Wall Street, Washington, and the Education of a President* (New York: Harper Collins, 2011), 4. (quoted below as *Suskind*)

[18] *Suskind*, 31.

[19] *Suskind*, 273.

[20] *Suskind*, 422.

and his guest speaker Wendy Edelberg. "Kreuger told the students that the class 'was an attempt to teach history in real time' and that they'd have to think clearly about distinguishing 'contributing factors from root causes.'"[21] Edelberg talked about the Financial Crisis Inquiry Commission's view of the matter, "focusing mostly on the financial industry's incentives and ultimately destructive activities, while she noted there was general disagreement that lack of regulation was a 'contributing factor more than a root cause.'"[22]

The effort of this little book is to get at, or rather get you at, the root cause, without massive ventures into contemporary and long-term history. I think now of one of the "Mensa murderers' row" mentioned above, Kenneth Rogoff, who was studiously into the 'long-term stuff' at the time of the White House meeting, and produced, with Carmen Reinhart, the 2010 book, *This Time Is Different: Eight Centuries of Financial Folly*. It caused a stir, yet its results, like those of the history portrayed in Piketty's *Capital in the Twenty-First Century*, are disputed, and in fact neither book leads anywhere near the core, the root cause, the seeds of a solution. Might there not be some gross folly at the heart of the whole pretentious pseudo-science of economics and its history?

---

[21] *Suskind*, 474.
[22] *Suskind*, 475.

INTRODUCTION

It seems odd yet useful for us here to begin by recalling two speeches of the first night of the Democratic Convention in Philadelphia, July 26th 2016, those of the senators Elizabeth Warren and Bernie Sanders. Warren spoke repeatedly of the "rigged system" that Trump exploited and supported; Bernie Sanders magnificently weaved his support of Hillary Clinton around his own push for a political revolution and economic justice, pausing over the wage problems of the middle-classes and indeed of life-unlivable on the $7.25-per-hour minimum wage. Late in the campaign Hillary talked of a minimum wage of $15. Donald Trump was not into such detail, but heavens he talked enough about rigged systems. Should I now, too, talk about rigged systems? Should I talk, as I hinted at the beginning of the Preface, about a quite different perspective on wages that in fact is excluded by the overall rigged system that I am opposing, that I am classifying as stupid? Had Trump lost the election we would certainly have heard a great deal about rigged systems. But now he moves on with some positivity and let us hope he keeps his promise and tackles—with serious consultations!—issues of serious American and Global concern. What I do not expect him to do is to side with me in tackling the massive rigged system that is present political economy, one that ignores the possibility of a science of economics that, among many other ills, is to promote a basic expansion that relates to a leap in basic wages and an intelligent reorientation of what I call *millionaire madness*.

My position is quite simply stated, and my inspiring authority for it revealed, when I give immediately a single quotation from the originator of the view I espouse. It mentions a basic economic expansion, and a second step in economic evolution, about both of which we shall muse later. But here you have it, written with the blunt confidence of a masterly innovative understanding.

> The difficulty emerges in the second step, the basic expansion. In equity it should be directed to raising the standard of living of the whole society. It does not. And the reason why it does not is not

the reason on which simple-minded moralists insist. They blame greed. But the prime cause is ignorance.[1]

It is not, then, the rigged system that is the grounding fault but a gross overall stupidity; it is not a matter of some tinkering round the problem of minimum or middle-class wages, but of a massive shift in wages blocked for centuries by a pseudo-scientific economics. Of course, there is a rigging that backs and sustains the pseudo-science, a "gentlemanly ring that conspires against the public,"[2] "the gullibility of society in accepting profit as a criterion of satisfactory enterprise."[3] Bernie Sanders was right on in mentioning the Koch brothers in his speech, but his own view is clouded by the cultural influences of their gentlemanly ring and the general gullibility associated with their outreach and the mood of present economics. Donald Trump now carries that culture into the Oval Office. So, I tackle the Oval Office. But not just because Donald is there. Why then? Well, we'll come to that later! The tricky issue, the issue of this little book, is the fixity of the economic stupidity that he embodies.

You have, I presume, already scanned the table of contents with its odd four parts. The oddness relates to the trickiness of dealing with the two central topics, profit and stupidity. I have been dealing with them in various ways for over forty years: but, as I struggle towards a fresh shot at that dealing, I see the story aspect of the problem as a distraction at this stage, even though it is pertinent to our struggle. So, I was led, putteringly, to juggle with the weave of topics in a manner that gestated into four parts. That juggling itself became intrusive as a topic in the Introduction, so that finally it seemed best eventually to underplay it and to simply invite you to plunge forward shortly into the first chapter after some short intimations of the content of the four parts of the book. Part One faces into the problem as uncomplicatedly as possible. The second part picks up on problems that emerge from relating that simple presentation of the core problem and its solution to present concrete global complexities. Part Three invites a distant

[1] Bernard Lonergan, *Macroeconomic Dynamics: An Essay in in Circulation Analysis*, edited by Frederick Lawrence, Patrick Byrne and Charles Hefling Jr., vol. 15, *Collected Works of Bernard Lonergan* (Toronto: University of Toronto Press, 1999), 82 (referred to later as *Macroeconomic Dynamics*).
[2] Bernard Lonergan, *For a New Political Economy*, edited by Philip McShane, vol. 21, *Collected Works of Bernard Lonergan* (Toronto: University of Toronto Press, 1998), 92 (referred to later as *For a New Political Economy*, and in chapter seven as **FNPE**).
[3] *Ibid*.

optimistic global view. The fourth part talks of facing the tasks of proximate implementation.

My ramblings so far are a success if you are now willing to have a shot at the climb beyond stupidity that is the journey of Part One, which does not push you to think in any vastly complex fashion: by the end you could have reached a quite simple beginning of the reach for a sane view of profit. Part Two launches into complexity of the economic view and of its origin; you might well prefer in a first read to skip to its final chapter, chapter 10, which invites a climb to a fuller if not yet fulsome view of profit. Part Three moves into glimpsing the view that is to mediate globally the hidden fulsomeness. The final part turns to the immediate circumstances, indeed to the core possibilities of the next four years of the reign of President Trump.

Finally, I would note that I have kept the climb strategically short. The four parts were, indeed, four volumes in the making, but my wish was to make the bones of a revolution descriptively and effectively available. The short introductions added here for each of the four parts will give further light on the strategy: the Epilogue will deal with the fullest context. I end, then, with a little enlargement of the description of the four parts. My first notion was to have these, separated, as introductions to those four parts: but it eventually seemed better to have them up front.

Part One, "Basics," begins with a first chapter reflection on the difficulty of getting to grips with a quite new view of economics and of profit, then moves in the second and third chapters to introducing that new view in two seemingly different ways. The first way simply moves from a standard diagram of economic flows to a diagram that represents the flows of money and goods that are integral to the study of a single, isolated economy. The second approach is more concrete in that it considers a major innovation in an island economy and arrives at a modest grasp of the fluctuations of production and of incomes that go with such an innovation. This musing over fluctuation gives a first idea of variations in the income called *profit*. The fourth chapter here tackles the question of the classifications that both underlie the previous chapters and give some idea of further complexities in classification. The fifth chapter, titled "Loose Ends," gives pointers both to looseness and indeterminacies that are to belong to serious scientific economics and to the looseness and vagueness that haunt these initial efforts to reach a new view. Finally, in the sixth chapter we tackle in a simple fashion the problem of formulating a satisfactory view of profit, one that explains profit as a feature in a coherent economics rather than it being assumed as a sort of dominant measure of economic success.

Part Two changes the pace, and deals with broader issues. The issue of international economics or of an economy open to patterns of trading, etc., was avoided in the Part One. The first two chapters here tackle the issues involved. But the approach is not elementary. An effort at elementary presentation of these aspects of the new economics would be counterproductive at this stage, like efforts to simplify the post-Newtonian physics of Einstein, Schrödinger, and Feynman. So, I draw on previous efforts, first, in chapter seven to indicate an imaging of global economic analysis that would hold together future empirical work, then, in the following chapter, to indicate, in a coherent fashion, how the elementary diagram of chapter two and three is to be extended to any nation's linking into the global economy.[4] Chapter nine then tackles the question of the origin of this new view of economics. It is a simple venture into the effort to meet the demand of the great economist and historian Joseph Schumpeter that economics be lifted from a flawed static analysis to a realistic dynamics of production. He writes of it as "crossing the Rubicon."[5] The demand was partially and vaguely met by Schumpeter himself but sublated into a coherent theory by Bernard Lonergan's work on the issue from 1929 to 1944. Against this background we have a final chapter of this part pushing for a fuller grip on the meaning of *profit*.

Part Three, "Remote Goals," moves towards intimating the distant collaborative context of economic studies, one that identifies the full collaboration as the emergence of what I call a positive Anthropocene Age beyond the negative perspective on this new ecological age given by such people as Roy Scranton and Ian Angus.[6] The new perspective is

---

[4] Chapter seven is identical with chapter three of my *Sane Economics and Fusionism* (Vancouver: Axial Publishing, 2010), 34–40. Chapter eight is identical with chapter four of the book referred to in note 5 of page ii above, *Economics for Everyone*. The word *identical* is used exactly. For example, I did not want to change terminology from the original presentations. Finding your way round different usages lifts the struggle to more serious levels of comprehension.

[5] "By the phrase, 'crossing the Rubicon,' I mean this: however important those occasional excursions into sequence analysis may have been, they left the main body of economic theory on the 'static' bank of the river; the thing to do is not to supplement static theory by the booty brought back from these excursions but to replace it by a system of general economic dynamics into which statics would enter as a special case." Joseph Schumpeter, *History of Economic Analysis* (Oxford: Oxford University Press, 1954), 1160.

[6] You had an initial meeting with Roy Scranton on page iii, at the end of note 7. Ian Angus also writes of the Anthropocene Age: *Facing the Anthropocene: Fossil*

conveniently and plausibly presented in chapter twelve, in the context of Wolf Blitzer's CNN program, *The Situation Room*. What emerges is the characterization of a full collaborative control of progress that involves an eightfold cyclic linkage of situation rooms that would allow a creative focus on any and all situations on the globe, large or small: a village in difficulty or a continent in distress. Chapters thirteen and fourteen fill out, in this larger context, aspects of economic control and behavior that need to be tackled if we are to move forward successfully: aspects that involve a fuller view of economic education, including an education regarding the corrupting and distracting tradings of the symbolic Wall Street. Think of that symbolism as including the IMF and the World Bank.

Part Four, "2020 Vision," returns to the realities of government and politics from which we took our start. What might we expect from Donald Trump regarding the shift to sanity? I sadly expect no encouragement from him in that direction. Still, there may be some bright folks in his administration. I suspect that there would have been larger possibilities with a Presidency of Hillary Clinton. But the democrats are not dead. There are relevant, in the sane economics that I advocate, strategies that would lift the democratic commitment to economic equality to new refinements, and indeed point to a larger fulfillment of Hillary's dream regarding the place of women in the economy as, in the future, moving us from negative to positive in the Anthropocene Age. Marxism, too, is to be salvaged. Chapter sixteen indicates how the salvaging involves a lift of serious thinking about that old Marxist slogan, "from each according to his ability, to each according to his needs." The final chapter points to the long-term hope for America and humanity that is to be associated with the new economic view.

Capitalism and the Crisis of the Earth System, with a foreword by John Bellamy Foster, Monthly Review Press, New York, 2016. Both authors will occupy us further, and the problems of the Anthropocene age, our present ecological age.

PART ONE

BASICS

1

Parallel Stupidities

There are many ways to begin our effort to identify the stupidity that concerns us in this little book. The stupidity is one of a backwardness grounded in error. Think of the mistake in astronomy of assuming that the sun moved round the earth. Think of the other stupidity in astronomy that held that the heavenly bodies were of a different matter than those found on earth. Or think of the mistake in chemistry, associated with the name *phlogiston*, that held sway for centuries. In all these cases the stupidity is identified best by finding out, at some level, what was missing, what was missed. What, then, is Donald missing when he thinks and talks of profit? I suppose that my simple and unhelpful answer can be that he, and our present culture, is missing the perspective that is introduced in chapter six and furthered in chapter ten. Another answer, not at all simple, is to drop the question mark in the question posed and make the odd, too-cute statement: **What** is Donald missing when he thinks and talks of profit.

This book deals with both answers in slow, introductory motions. Let me divert about this slowness of the revolution of whatting and thinking that is needed.

I recall, as I start, my source for the revolution, Bernard Lonergan, writing in the early 1940s of "readaptation of the whole existing structure,"[1] of "a new order."[2] He wrote of the need to "descend to familiar things . . . in quite an unfamiliar fashion."[3] Here I wish you to self-protectively and encouragingly think of other stupidities in the history of understanding and so finding for yourself helpful parallels to our problem as well as grounds for self-excusing.

The easiest paralleling comes with humor. I think of the story of the elegant leisured gentleman in Princeton who met Einstein casually and was quite pleased that, since they both had an interest in music, the great man accepted an invitation to tea. All went well in the shared world of music until

---

[1] Bernard Lonergan, *For a New Political Economy*, 6.

[2] *Ibid.*, 4.

[3] *Ibid.*, 8.

the gentleman startled Einstein with the request that Einstein explain his theory of relativity: "but please, in my own simple words: I have no head for equations."

The joke goes further. Did Einstein falter? Did, later, Stephen Hawking falter? Both men did; both men attempted what is expressed nicely in French as *haute vulgarization*. But Hawking's faltering was deeper, yet strangely suggestive. "The basic ideas about the origin and fate of the universe can be stated without mathematics in a form that people without a scientific education can understand."[4] The character of the strange suggestiveness is to emerge as we ramble together in and around the seventeen chapters of this little book.

Now I must immediately note that I do not expect Donald Trump to take me with full seriousness.[5] The best that I can hope for is that some few, be they in his administration or not, catch on to the core flaw that haunts the policies and practices and detailed dynamics of his government, and related financial institutions, corporations, unions, whatever. [6] (Did I mention economics departments?!)

Indeed, I hope that a pragmatic realism would lead the Republicans to the task of catching on to the core and its consequences as a way towards a second term of power. Might they not suspect that pushing towards the identification of the flaw, if not its elimination, would boost their electability? But I would prefer to think that there are some among both parties who will come to recognize the flaw as a massive, pretentious sickness of global thinking and who will dream and scream effectively of the new culture that would follow its elimination. (Dream on Phil!)

"But," you rightly ask, "What is the flaw?"

During these past decades I have tried various ways of stirring that rightly-asking towards fermenting an ethos of asking slowly and seriously about its nature and its effects. I will weave those various ways into my

---

[4] Stephen Hawking, *A Brief History of Time: From Big Bang to Black Holes* (New York: Bantham Books, 1988), 6.

[5] We remain in the world of humor here as I point you to thinking of Plato's shot at educating the ruler Dionysius 2484 years ago: you might follow this up by now reading pages 89–90 below. Dionysius is replaced by an American President.

[6] *Core* is a key word here, and a focus of chapters 10 and 12 below. I would note that I am pointing towards something deeply novel. This is not just a revamping of Joel Bakan. See his *The Corporation: The Pathological Pursuit of Profit and Power* (New York: Free Pres, 2004).

present effort in an improved strategy that just might get to a core-showing of the flaw, and of its global solution, on the road.

Perhaps noting one cluster of effects expressed in the 2016 election campaign would encourage a serious start among a few, particularly some few economists and journalists. Both candidates weaved together broad policy perspectives regarding income inequality. On my view, that weaving and suggesting is of no more serious significance than Piketty's pointing to a solution through the taxation of the monied class. Piketty showed no suspicion of the need of getting to the heart of the matter.

"What is the heart of the matter?" you may now honestly and impatiently repeat in your rightly asking. And I feel the need to temper your impatience with some further humor. I could take any of the mistakes mentioned in my first paragraph above, and talk of people living with a flaw for centuries, even millennia, but perhaps it is easiest on the imagination to take time over, or with, that very bright guy Isaac Newton. So, we get ourselves into his puzzling mood under the apple tree. What was his puzzle? Here I wish you to relax into whatever level of that puzzling that you are comfortable with. Take the puzzle at its lightest. Here you are, lying back in the grass, looking up through the leaves of the apple tree at the moon. An apple or three fall, and then the really odd question ferments in your brain: Why does not the moon fall?

Notice how the odd question is odd in that you may never have thought of it before, and indeed you may find it hard to take it as a serious question even now. Furthermore, if you take it seriously, you still might come at it from such a context and perspective that you get nowhere. We could be distracted here into musing about *The Sleepwalkers*,[7] but best stay in our ballpark by returning again to a twisted parallel with Piketty's puzzling. Why don't the monied "fall"? You may think of the rest of us, Johnny and Jane Appleseeds falling in the sense of the growing income gap. But now there can emerge a new level of questioning the gap. Can? Aye, there's the rub! The new level of questioning may not emerge: the easier stance is to take a gap for granted and try for a practical way to make it less painful, or even make it a little less of a gap. But what of the odd questions: Why doesn't the moon fall? Why don't the monied fall?

---

[7] I am recalling the suggestive title of Arthur Koestler's big and successful 1959 book about astronomy. The subtitle was, *A History of Man's Changing Vision of the Universe*. As we shall glimpse, especially in chapters 12, 13, and 17, it will take a very slow collaborative climb to talk effectively about and to our Anthropocene times.

Think of these questions as ideas, ideas that I ask you to pause over. But the asking needs to become a real effective nudging in you, a molecular mood fermented by a societal evolution. Joan Robinson tries for such a fermenting by her peculiar "starting-over" in the first sentences of her *Freedom and Necessity.* "Consider the profiles of a dolphin and a herring. The resemblance between them consists in each being well suited to swimming. The evolutionary relationship between them is extremely remote."[8] On she goes then, through a dense history of commerce and money, to touch down on the problem of profiteering in her final chapter. She gets nowhere, yet there she is, brilliant in her version of the stupidity I am talking about.

How can I invite you to take a different evolutionary route, or even a route that avoids digging round in evolution's twists? I am desperately trying to sow effectively the idea of the question that brings us to face the character of the flaw in a long history of thinking about commerce. Robinson helps me here as I go back from her first chapter to her frontispiece from Mao Tse-tung: "Where do ideas come from? Do they drop from the skies? No. Are they innate in the mind? No. They come from social practice."

It is quite amazing how we miss that pointer of Mao. We regularly lift social practice into conventional realms of thinking about it. I recall now with sad amusement my last effort—a few years ago—at presenting the way beyond conventional stupidity to an economics department in the State University of an Asian capital, whose country I leave unnamed. The question session was warming up in identifying levels of bafflement till one of the professors posed the question, "But is it not all in Mankiw?"[9] My response began, "Well, if you really think that, we have nothing to discuss." It was, alas, sadly true, we really were not on the same page. My page was that of the sight of a side-street barber who had only a chair and a scissors doing, so-to-speak, a capital job on a consumer. The department's page was a leaf from Mankiw.

---

[8] *Freedom and Necessity: An Introduction to the Study of Society* (New York: Vintage, 1971), 9.

[9] Gregory Mankiw's text, *Principles of Economics*, is in its seventh edition. It is used worldwide. For a detailed critique of it see Bruce Anderson and Philip McShane, *Beyond Establishment Economics: No Thank You, Mankiw* (Halifax: Axial Publishing, 2002).

2

THE KEY DIAGRAM

So I begin by taking a leaf out of Mankiw's text, the leaf that contains his fundamental diagram of single-economy circulation. The diagram is repeated in various forms throughout his text. Indeed, it can be found in any text of economics, what I identify and sketch below in its simplest form, the household-to-firm diagram.

In another introductory text I give various versions of it, versions that include banking, taxing, even moving beyond to the relating of economies.[1] But let me not distract you here with complications. We try for a first step towards a new science of economics by plunging into the presentation that I have used as a beginning in recent years. I quote from a previous work, then return, at the conclusion of that presentation and your efforts with regard to it, to the task of fuller contextualizations.

The Key Diagrams[2]

We start now with the standard diagram of current economic texts and move fairly smoothly to a diagram that points to that new science of economics that is to save us from global disaster. I wish you to come with me slowly and quietly from the standard diagram, through two transition diagrams, to the central scientific diagram of future economics.

We start with the standard Household to Firm diagram of the first weeks of elementary economics, with the obvious meanings for the symbols of Households, Firms, income, and demand:

---

[1] The introductory text, referred to already but best named again here is Philip McShane, *Economics for Everyone: Das Jus Kapital* (Vancouver: Axial Publishing, 1998).
[2] Philip McShane, *Piketty's Plight and the Global Future* (Vancouver: Axial Publishing, 2014), 11–14.

There is an easy way to add the second type of firm, which supplies not consumer goods, but stuff for the first type of firm: maintenance and innovative stuff, which I'll symbolize as m_i. (Think of **m** as pointing to maintenance and more!! I am thinking of innovation of course.) Here you are:

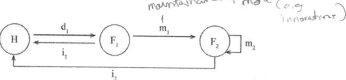

Notice now that F_2 is in the same boat as F_1 as regards maintenance and innovation. But we don't want to add F_3, F_4 ... I won't go into the simplification of packing in all the series of F_n into F_2. I just claim here that it works empirically as grounding decent measurements of business flows.

But how do we get that into the diagram?

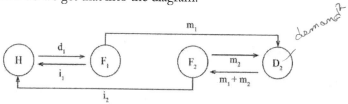

We can make this neater by thinking of two types of demand and, if you wish, replacing H (Households) by D_1, with flow d_1 and making, e.g., d_2-type flowings from D_2, the demand of firms for capital stuff, marked in the diagram as m_2. Next, we find that we get a more workable diagram by laying the transactions out in a square and adding the flow lines:

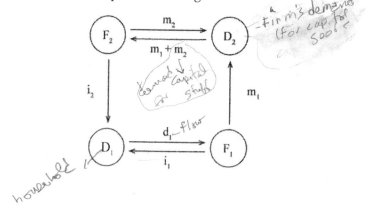

8

This would be the beginnings of a new economics of measurable flows, one that would yield norms of financing, of profit in both normal and innovative economies, etc., etc.[3]

The Full Diagram[4]

The total of initial payments, income, is clearly identical with total outlay in the chosen interval. DI' + DI" = DO' + DO". But now I would ask you to put aside other problems and pause over the notion of **crossover**. We are back, but freshly, at the diagram at the end of the previous page, pushing you to settle into the diagram of the page to follow here. A firm's outlay involves a split: instead of the **i** and **m** of the first diagram I note that split, in the second diagram, as a fractional split of DO. In the next chapter we shall connect the split and its complexities to innovation as well as maintenance, but here stay with the 'static-dynamic' of a fixed economy. Then, we think of G' as the fraction of outlay that goes to maintenance in a basic firm. A quirk of symmetry leads to using (1 – G") as the fraction of outlay that goes to maintenance in surplus business: Then you have

---

[3] And I should add here—see the following note on the problem of compactness and incompleteness—a note, a high note indeed, a high 'see', relating to the suggestion about wages in the second paragraph of the Preface. There are to emerge shocking norms of workers' incomes. It is amazing how we have gone on so long accepting putterings and utterings about minimum or living wages. But there is a long history to this that would sublate Piketty's hefty analysis: tricky work that involves the difficult shift to two-flow analysis.

[4] *Piketty's Plight and the Global Future*, 43–44. I decided to carry forward here rather abruptly. See note 7 below on a classroom version of the initial topic. My problem throughout the book is the avoidance of detail such as was mentioned in the previous note. My experience of tutoring this stuff to individuals is that one needs the sort of detail that the last note pointed to, and details, e.g., how to think out transition payments, half-made goods, etc., and the manner in which business people handle turnover lengths of production in figuring out financing and credit. My problem brings to mind Bernard Lonergan, in his last years, getting serious about an introductory text. I am led to quote my conclusion (p. xxxi) to my lengthy Introduction to *For a New Political Economy*: "Certainly, the work of the last years of his life included pointers towards an introductory primer. But the massively innovative primers that would meet millennial needs, 500-page texts of empirically rich, locally orientated, normatively focused non-truncated writing, are distant probabilities." Added there, ending the Introduction, is a note on textbook traditions. At all events, I risk adding a dense completeness to this short chapter, and variations in terminology. But the key point has already been made: the need for a big empirical leap beyond the single flow analysis, to a double flow analysis.

9

crossover-ratios G' and G" for the two circuits, G' being for basic-circuit maintenance and G" being for surplus-circuit wages. These are to be, of course, zones of focused interest in future empirical economics.

Finally, I add into the diagram the redistribution function that I associate with secondhand trading, but think of it now in terms of money flows, which I simply mark into my diagram as four lines outgoing from the redistribution area: D', S', D", S". I put that diagram in here immediately. It is my version of the final diagram concocted by Lonergan in 1944.[5]

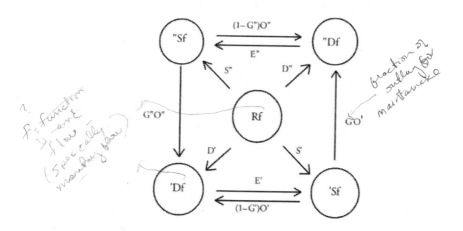

Such is my presentation from *Piketty's Plight and the Global Future*. In pushing on towards what I call the final diagram of Lonergan's single economy without trans-national trade I know that I have pushed too hard, given you too much to get a grip on without a great deal of illustrative work. So I would ask you to focus on the simple aspect of the elementary diagram that allows you to do what I call the reversed Newtonian jump.

Think, now, as I suggested in chapter one, of being under the apple tree, locked into a long-established culture—it is a matter of images, of neurodynamics[6]—where you think of the movements of earthly bodies as different from heavenly bodies: 2 sets of laws, of rules. Getting the bright idea that there is only one set of rules: that would be, and indeed was, the

---

[5] The diagram appears on page 258 of Bernard Lonergan, *For a New Political Economy*.

[6] We touch on that topic further as we go along, especially in chapter 13, "The Faculty of Culture." But there is no harm in you pausing now over the notion that the dynamic patterns of your cranial molecules can be locked into a view.

beginning of quite a shake-up. Perhaps it is useful to pause here over a therapeutic parallel. Your therapist gets you to a basic insight: it is quite another to get that insight effectively into one's nerves. In the economic case there is an accepted culture of there being one flow of goods and money from which laws have to be developed. What a jump it is psychically to the insight that there are two flows! Psychically? What I call the intussusception of the two flows as dominating one's further thinking comes only as one pushes on into the strange new world.

I do not wish to enlarge on any of that in this introductory chapter. The next chapter introduces a helpful illustration and, speaking from my own experience of struggling into this strange realism, and from teaching it at different levels, one must ramble back and forth, puzzling concretely over real situations. I recall now one experience of teaching a grade 12 economics class where I used very successfully stories of my own teen-years, working in a small bakery owned by my father: you might find it a useful back-up to this compact chapter.[7] Furthermore, you'll find yourself puzzled over the various connecting lines in the full diagram and the distinctions that are implicit there. Especially tricky is the zone that I have left very much in the air, the zone named by the symbol Rf, which stands for "redistribution function." You may think of it as the world of banking, but it is in fact a large mad contemporary world that includes the goings-on symbolized by the name *Wall Street*.[8] For the present it is enough for you to hold to the notion that the four symbols S', D', S'', D'', refer to flows to and fro from banks to respective areas in the economy, as well as flows of secondhand trading. Think, for instance, of D' coming to the $'Df$ (read the three components of the symbol as "basic demand function") from Rf as a loan for buying a house.

---

[7] The lecture is reproduced as chapter one, "The Key Elementary Class," in my *Sane Economics and Fusionism* (Vancouver: Axial Publishing, 2010).

[8] You might, at some stage, like some background on Wall Street: see Jeffrey Little and Lucien Rhodes, *Understanding Wall Street* (New York: McGraw Hill, 5th edition, 2010). For an up-to-date relevant comment on this mad world, see Mervyn King, *The End of Alchemy: Money, Banking, and the Future of the Global Economy* (New York: W.W. Norton, 2016). Neither book is in our ballpark. For further comments on King's book, see note 7 of chapter 4 below, page 20.

3

INVENTING THE PLOUGH

We proceed now to exercise the imagination. My suggestion here is one that occurred to me, as it were, on the imaginative-challenge spot in a puzzled Californian gathering on economics over thirty years ago: they just could not get the point of oscillations in consumer prices caused by innovations. I suppose the nudge came from my Celtic background and indeed planting potatoes by hand, but I placed the relevant goings-on in a story of the Canadian Maritimes, a story of Prince Edward Island. For Chinese audiences there is a long history of the invention and modification of the plough. But what is key is pushing oneself to concrete imaging. Perhaps readers in the U.S. would think of settlers in Idaho with an interest in potato-growing who had wagoned there—stretch your fantasy, leave Kansas—arriving without a plough culture.

On our fictitious island we assume an essentially stable culture of eating and drinking, learning and laughing. But your assumption of it needs leisured pauses, even flights of fancy. There is no need to bring in any serious economic history or theory. If you wish for a larger context for my little set of suggestions you will find that a previous effort has that little suggestive set on page 19 of a fairly lengthy—pages 15–38—chapter titled "Baskets and Handfills," the title recalling a more primitive cultural innovation.[1] Let me quote the beginning of that effort immediately, thus nudging you to fancy some local parallels that may help.

> We might well have taken for our island Prince Edward Island, famous for its potatoes, or Ireland, at some early part of an imagined history. But let us settle for the very small isolated island of Atlantis where, as our story begins, there is cultivation of the

---

[1] The previous effort is my *Economics for Everyone* mentioned regularly already. The fruit-gathering illustration is worth following up. Michael Shute has a magnificent detailed discussion of the invention by a fishing community of a weir: "Real Economic Variables," *Divyadaan: Journal of Education and Philosophy*, vol. 21, no. 2, 2010, 183–94. This entire volume would be a helpful acquisition. I was guest editor and gave it the general title, "Do You Want a Sane Global Economics?"

soil by spade, as well as village leisure in horse-racing, island transport by horse-cart, but no plough. Still, there is a tavern in the town, and the story opens therein with a group round a table that includes a lady, named Joey for she is a central character, who owns the main horse-stable, the gent who runs the local primitive bank, and a potato-farmer. As you get the point of the story you can add in other suitable characters: the blacksmith, the owner of the leather store, etc.

After some intake of the popular intoxicant, made from potatoes of course (In Ireland we call it *poiteen*. Sometimes we allow it to age up to 48 hours: how about that for turnover frequency![2]), the talk turns towards potato-cultivation. Such is the popularity of the racetrack, gambling, manufacturing ornaments, weaving intricate clothes, brewing and consuming poiteen, etc., that the farmer has a problem finding good help. The upshot of the discussion and the ferment is that—eureka!—the horse-owner gets the grand idea that if the farmer's spade could somehow be angled behind the horse and pulled by the horse, it would upgrade and up-pace the tilling. And, of course, it would be good for both their businesses.[3]

The banker looks Joey in the eye and uses a typically Irish expression in a nicely ambiguous sense: "I have to give you credit for that"![4]

---

[2] The question of turnover frequency and turnover magnitude is a key issue in working out credit. We shall meet it again as we move along. But you might find it interesting to check economic text-books. You will notice that there is no entry in their indices under *turnover*. Perhaps you might be positively and constructively distracted here to think out, with Bernard Lonergan, the various paces at which ships can be constructed. See Lonergan, *For a New Political Economy*, 260–63. Check the index under *turnover* for fuller enlightenment.

[3] *Economics for Everyone*, 19.

[4] This is a very Irish way of speaking that goes quite beyond banking. It is a meaning regularly missing in modern financial transactions. It is worthwhile quoting Schumpeter on the matter. "It should be observed how important it is for the system of which we are trying to construct a model, that the banker should know, and be able to judge, what his credit is used for and that he should be an independent agent. To realize that is to understand what banking means." *Business Cycles: A Theoretical, Historical, and Statistical Analysis of the Capitalist Process* (New York: McGraw Hill, 1939), vol. 1, 116. "The banker's function is essentially a critical, checking, admonitory one. Alike in this respect to economists, bankers are

In footnote 4 I mentioned Schumpeter's massive two-volume effort to enlighten economists on the story of business cycles. In a much earlier brilliant little work he gives a more focused account of the temporal patterns of innovation.[5] We just can't go there in this little venture. What I need from you is an effort to come to grips with a few broad transitions. The innovation calls for, calls forth, credit, from the island banker(s). There is a subtly-patterned surge of the production of ploughs. With a lag of perhaps a couple of years,[6] a plough culture comes to be, with a larger flow of goods like potatoes. Gradually a new dynamic stability is reached. You are, I hope, at least vaguely with me here. Might you have a shot at making sense of the goings-on by means of the diagram with its cross-overs? We have, in our little concrete model, three stages: there is a surplus surge, then a basic surge, followed by a return to an equilibrium state.[7] Much later in your thinking you

---

worth their salt only if they make themselves thoroughly unpopular with governments, politicians, and the public. That does not matter in times of intact capitalism. In the times of decadent capitalism this piece of machinery is likely to be put out of gear by legislation." *Ibid.*, 118. I am re-quoting Schumpeter from a fuller consideration of the topic in chapter 6, "Proximate Pragmatics," in my *Pastkeynes Pastmodern Economics: A Fresh Pragmatism* (Halifax: Axial Publishing, 2002).

[5] Joseph A. Schumpeter, *The Theory of Economic Development: An Inquiry into Profits, Capital, Credit, Interest, and the Business Cycle*, translated from the German (1911) by Redvers Opie, with a new Introduction by John E. Elliott, 16th printing (London: Transaction Publishers, 2012).

[6] This is a challenge to your imagination, but obviously it pushes the scientific community towards empirical details of productive processes. Such an enterprise is magnificently illustrated by Joseph Schumpeter's two-volume work on *Business Cycles* mentioned in note 4 above.

[7] I slip in here words unfamiliar to you, used technically by Lonergan. The word *surplus* may bring to mind Marx on surplus value etc., but I would have you think more of Toynbee's historical notion of withdrawal to return, creative pausing towards betterment. In this little book I must needs skim along. See, for example, the final skimming past issues of surplus, values, income inequalities, etc. in note 15 of the Epilogue, pages 141–42 below. For the moment, think of the credit—in all senses—given to the innovator. The surge, grounded in the full sense of credit, grounds also an increase of income: things are moving better. There are repayments involved, but the innovator's credit is honored by a lift in standard of living which may not be proportionate because of an acknowledged hierarchy of involvement. There is surplus income thus divided, but there is also an odd reality which Lonergan writes of thus in 1944: "pure surplus income is at the nerve center of free economies." *For a New Political Economy*, 294. He had introduced his meaning of surplus in the earlier 1942 version of his analysis, "Theorem of the

will see, seize, be seized by, the diagram in a fashion that fits your achievement of imagining, especially if you have concrete parallels that help you imagine the shifting of a community through the rhythms. A musician might think of paging through presentations of Chopin's Mazurka's or the text of songs by the Beatles: you fly way beyond the print. Look again at the complete diagram before we move on: is it less mysterious than when you first read chapter two?

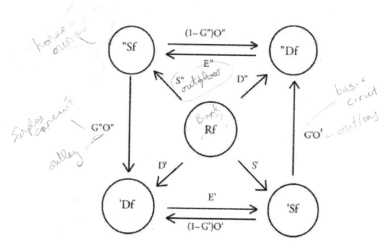

The first surging stage pivots on the outflow, S", from banks to the group around Joey, the innovative horse-owner. There is an initiation of a build-up of the set of goings-on forming the group of industries that are to provide the full reality of a horse trekking along a field towing a plough. Flex your imagination to view tanners and blacksmiths, etc., etc. But the core point here, the troublesome point, is the wisdom of the community regarding the increase income that boosts G"O". A burst of spending the

Surplus" (*ibid.*, 49–50), where he talks of "a flow of income beyond all cost of living, all taxes and charities, all maintenance and replacement: it is net surplus, an excess profit that can be spent only by being invested." *Ibid.*, 50. This is deep water that we are not entering here. My effort is directed to getting a beginning of cultural sanity seeded: the acknowledgment of the scientific significance of a two-flow analysis.

extra wages would nudge up prices of a non-increasing supply of consumer goods.[8]
    Were I to share with you the leads to your efforts here, this chapter would be at least fifty pages long. Perhaps that paradoxically makes the point to me that I should cut my hints to a minimum?[9] There is the slow emergence of the ploughing unit, leading to its purchase and use, the leveling off of its production, the leveling off of the increased flow of products leading to a new level dynamics of goods and services. And, there is the counter-flow of money that ends, too, in a new level: should I mention measures of GDP? Then I must add the puzzle that it is no longer GDP but GDP' and GDP".
    The end product of the innovative complex is a new standard of living, including—here a topic for serious creative musing—a new standard of leisure. All this has its monetary equivalent, and the nudge to that equivalence is seeded in the reality intended by the banker in his simple statement to Joey: "I have to give you credit for that." What is the meaning of "have to" there? Might I suggest that it is a balanced, indeed, wise, promise weaved into the occurrence of Joey's idea? Forty years ago I began a relevant chapter on "The Economy of Truth"[10] by quoting the economist Robert Heilbroner: "Behind all the symbols, however, rests the central requirement of faith. Money serves its indispensable purposes as long as we believe in it.

---

[8] This tricky point was the central topic in a newspaper article written by Lonergan in 1941, during the Second World War (*The Montreal Beacon*, 7 February 1941). The title was "Savings Certificates and Catholic Action." The essay is available in his *Collected Works, CWL* 20, *Shorter Papers*. Perhaps a quotation might help. "What is the motive for saving? It is our principle of **superflua status**, surplus income. Such surplus income is beyond one's reasonable requirements for a standard of living. But plainly the one and a half thousand millions generated by our war effort are surplus income: they are in excess of the three thousand millions generated by the ordinary economy; they cannot be spent on consumer goods; they cannot belong to any individual's standard of living. They happen to come to individuals, because that is the nature of the exchange system. But their function is to pay for the war effort, for that is the nature of the circulation. Etc." *CWL* 20, 72.

[9] I muse over the problem of summary in chapter five and on strategies of hinting in chapter fourteen, when I talk of COPON.

[10] It is chapter seven of a small book of the early 1970s, very relevant to our topic, Philip McShane, *Wealth of Self and Wealth of Nations: Self-Axis of the Great Ascent* (Washington, DC: University Press of America, 1975). This book is available at: http://www.philipmcshane.org/published-books.

It ceases to the moment we do not. Money has been called the promise men live by."[11]

The last sentence there will occupy us variously as we struggle on here and indeed on into this millennium. What is a promise? What is it to give credit? Who profits from the idea and the innovation? The banker, or those around him in my imagined Irish pub, might well have nodded communally, even raised a glass, as someone among them said, "*das jus Kapital*," a Dublin-speak way of killing the "th" and dropping a "t" from *just* in a manner that invites Marx into our tavern.[12] And was it not Marx who said, "Outside of a dog a book is a man's best friend. Inside a dog it is too dark to read."[13] Inside the present stupid economic culture there is an idiot scientifically ungrounded dogma about profit that makes it too dark for us, and for Donald, and—most of all—for professors of economics, to read.

---

[11] Robert Heilbroner, *The Economic Problem* (Englewood Cliffs, NJ: Prentice-Hall, 1972), 352.

[12] *Economics for Everyone: Das Jus Kapital* has this trickery in the subtitle.

[13] It was, of course, the other Marx.

4

CLASSIFICATIONS

What is amazing—or what will be amazing when you look back, or forward, at the end of this initial effort to brood over the Right Stuff—is the foggy muddles of definitions that survive and control the mess of economic pseudo-science, whether one considers Capitalism or Marxism. Such fogginess of establishment American economics was the topic of *Beyond Establishment Economics: No Thank You, Mankiw*.[1] But Marxism does no better, and I might well have taken such a classic text as John Eaton's *Political Economy: A Marxist Textbook*, and work it as Anderson and I did with the book of Mankiw.[2] Eaton, like Robinson, takes an evolutionary run at the topic, but putters along, as does Marx, with conventional descriptive distinctions that keep the fog quite stable. There is the problem—recall Piketty—of the increasing incomes of the capitalist owners and the 'mean' fixity of the exploited workers. As Robinson remarked, in her gallant little rejected text, "it is time to go back to the beginning and start again."[3]

But before I invite us to do that regarding classification, I would note a further way of taking the advice of a fresh start. There are now, in the U.S., two political parties with their histories.[4] My interest here is in the origins of these parties and their political bents. One can track back to 1794, move on

---

[1] See above, at note 9, page 6.

[2] I was nudged towards this crazy notion by musing over Eaton's lightweight reflections on profit. The Mankiw book had the terrible rhyming subtitle, "No Thank You, Mankiw." What might I say to Eaton? "No Heat On, Eaton." Marxism is no more viable or sane than present capitalism. On the muddled middle road of socialism see Ian Angus, *Facing the Anthropocene: Fossil Capitalism and the Crisis of the Earth System* (New York: Monthly Review Press, 2016).

[3] Joan Robinson and John Eatwell, *An Introduction to Modern Economics* (New York: McGraw Hill, 1973), 52.

[4] There have been, of course, other ventures in leadership over the centuries and even at present. As it happens, I type this on the morning of August 3, 2016, with the excitement of looking forward to watching the Libertarian appeal, later in the day, for a place in the election. They found their place, as did Jill Stein.

through the nineteenth century, etc., and arrive at their present platforms. Those platforms are Mankiw-flavored, even if in a foggy scatty undefined way.[5] Might we get the politicians to go back to their beginnings, prior to the stale fixity of one-flow economics with its back against the Wall Street sickness, and find that they can arrive at a defined political stand—No thank you Mankiw—by associating that stand with a precisely defined and invitingly operable democratic economic science?

But to do that there has to emerge a core devoted to serious thinking about that new beginning. Might there be a few of Bernie Sander's disappointed followers up to such a focus?[6] Certainly such a focus—I describe it particularly in chapters ten and fourteen—would be better than "occupying Wall Street" anew or hanging round the gates of the lofty international gatherings tinkering with finances and trade.[7]

It is not a matter, for example, of property possession, of us against them, of capitalist versus worker, of Wall Street battering Main Street, but a matter of finding normative flows of the two types of income involved in mirroring the rhythms of production. This, I would surmise, is quite a leap

---

[5] Mankiw had been occasionally mistaken for a Democrat but he cleared that up on his blog exactly 10 years ago. And he was also a member of Bush's administration. So he bridges nicely both platforms.

[6] The importation of Bernie Sander's perspective into the present administration is something worth watching. My interest in this little book are the questions of inequality he raises as only the surface of much larger issues whose grounds are in the muddle that at present passes for economic science.

[7] In note 8 of chapter two (p. 11) I mentioned Mervyn King's, *The End of Alchemy: Money, Banking, and the Future of the Global Economy* (New York: W.W. Norton, 2016). It is useful at this stage to pause over his work, sad because, for all its present acclaim, it is really a foggy tinkering dominated by conventional thinking. His Introduction echoes my aim in this book. "Unless we go back to the underlying causes we will never understand what happened and will be unable to prevent a repetition and help our economies truly recover." He weaves his way eruditely through recent financial messings and comes up finally with his lame view of banking as "pawnbroker for all seasons." *Ibid.*, 270–81. Recalling my plough parable of the previous chapter, I would note that he too has a "parable of financial markets on a desert island" (145–48) but it settles into the same unrealism that haunted Keynes and that persists in neoclassical economics. Like Robinson— a colleague of King's at Cambridge—he had his doubts about the obscurities in Keynes, and in particular acknowledges the general failure to account for booms and slumps. Chapters 3, 4, and 7 ramble towards (the title of chapter 7) "Innocence Regained: Reforming Money and Banking." The innocence he regains and promotes weaves round his innocence of the missing science of economics.

for you, a leap quite beyond John Eaton and Mankiw, beyond Samuelson, Kalecki, Robinson, and Eichner.[8] But perhaps you might glimpse the beginnings by noting that wage-earners buy shares,[9] and tycoons drink cocktails. The cross-overs of the basic diagram are a reality that needs precise classification and detection if we are to get from the flat-earth society of present party politics, economic putterings, global financial bumblings and gamblings, to sanely operating scientific economics.

I wish to talk a little more about classification, but it seems worthwhile to point, in note 10, to a massive heuristic shift based on a precise constellation of scientific classifications. That shift is an analysis of the cycles of accurately-identified layers of basic incomes and of surplus incomes that might be associated with the simple instance of plough-invention sketched in the previous chapter. The analysis is in startling correspondence with the oscillations and crises dealt with by Joseph Schumpeter's treatment of three small cycles, named *Kitchins*, in the large cycle of 9–10 years named a *Juglar*.[10]

---

[8] I end my random list of honest searchers with Alfred Eichner whose remark I regularly recall: "Late in the day, after they have had a few drinks, many economic professors will begin to admit to their own reservations about the theory which forms the core of the economic curriculum." Eichner, *A Guide to Post-Keynesian Economics* (White Plains, NY: M. E. Sharpe, 1979), vii. The three prior names in my list are of people who struggled in various positive ways towards the science of economics about which I write here.

[9] The issue of investments, shares, corporations' responsibilities, etc., etc. is a topic way beyond our short ramble. I referred earlier here (note 6, p. 4) to Joel Bakan, *The Corporation: The Pathological Pursuit of Profit and Power* (New York: The Free Press, 2004). See also Bruce Anderson, "The Fifth Functional Specialty and Foundations for Corporate Law and Governance Policies," in *Seeding Global Collaboration*, edited by Patrick Brown and James Duffy (Vancouver: Axial Publishing, 2016), 115–128. But closer to our topic is an appeal Lonergan was in the habit of making during the war years of the early 1940s: See, e.g., "Saving Certificates and Catholic Action," *Shorter Papers*, CWL 20 (Toronto: University of Toronto Press, 2007), 68–73, which I referred to already in note 8 of page 16. "War activity generates another one and a half thousand millions in income; for it to do so continuously without causing a disastrous inflation, it too must flow back to its source. But the problem is, how effect this return flow? ... It is easy to construct a big net to catch big fish, but, when most of the fish are small, what is needed is a big net to catch little fish." *Ibid.*, 70. The deep problem is to have a cultural net that is not just bureaucratic tinkering.

[10] *For a New Political Economy*, chapter 18, "Cycles of Incomes and Prices," 285–307. The parallel of the two analyses is pointed out on page 306, and I may as well quote here the full reference I gave there: Joseph Schumpeter, *Business Cycles: A*

My problem here is to get you focused on the relevant classifications and avoid giving you an impression of the shift being obvious but irrelevant. So, I pointed forward in the previous paragraph and its note 10 to the manner in which the simple classification we dealt with in chapters two and three leads to a massive lift in business cycle analysis. This may not impress you: you may even think that such analysis is only of historical interest, something that belonged to major innovations of global consequence, inventions of ploughs or trains.[11] In that case, perhaps a pause over the Anthropocene crisis can nudge you into interest, for it is very difficult to take an intelligent stand against that crisis calling for massive innovations that will indeed push us into such analyses as those of Schumpeter and Kondratieff. But my invitation to pause has another twist. It is the twist that may lift you to glimpse that the classification distinction that emerges from chapter two and three is the key to meeting that crisis of what I call a turn from negative Anthropocene humanism to a permanent positive Anthropocene age of later millennia. Of the very recent book by Ian Angus, *Facing the Anthropocene: Fossil Capitalism and the Crisis of the Earth System*, Mike Davis has written, "crisp, eloquent and deeply informed."[12] Yet Ian Angus does not even brush past this central problem of the shift, the problem of two-layered shifts in production and promise, the problem of the **what** in all of us that grounds the fresh meaning of money and promise. Here is not the place to enter into Angus's eloquent plea,[13] but perhaps it might nudge you and annoy him to think of the title of another book: *Profit: The Stupid View of Ian Angus*.

Theoretical, Historical, and Statistical Analysis of the Capitalist Process (New York: McGraw-Hill, 1939; paperback ed., 1964; original German, two volumes, 1939), 170–73.

[11] The climate change problem is pushing towards the need for a bubbling of ideas regarding proximate and distant innovations. Cycles such as the long cycle called Kondratieff may be a normality of these next millennia: how are we to handle them so that they are not booms and busts? But on my mind as I write is Alvin Hansen addressing the American Economic Association in the late 1930s, when Schumpeter's two volumes on *Business Cycles* appeared (see the previous note), presenting the view that business cycle theory was a thing of the past.

[12] I quote from the top of the 2016 paperback cover of Angus's book. Mike Davis is an activist student of urbanization, with such works to his credit as *Planet of Slums* (New York: Verso, 2006).

[13] It is eloquent and, as Ian Angus pushes towards his conclusion, he is indeed making the same case as Lonergan did in the conclusion of chapter seven of *Insight*, the need for some type of Cosmopolis. But his bent is towards some type of

At all events, after tossing round possible enlargements on the problem of classification, it seems to me that it is best in this chapter on classification not to enter into some summary presentation,[14] but to leave you, first and most importantly, to brood further over my simple pointers of chapters two and three. That brooding will, I hope, lead you to sympathize with my obscure pointing, through this chapter and in the two dense chapters to follow: a psychically unsatisfactory pointing to the panoply of complexifications that dance on the simple distinction of two flows of goods and money.

You may well, as I would hope, rise to glimpse these complexifications by a persistent concrete imaging of actual production and sales. In doing that, indeed, you will leave the usual textbook literature behind. Innovating in a business pushes the innovator into considerations of turnover, its magnitude, and its frequency: if you can't tighten frequency sufficiently your financing may knock you out of business. But where is that problem handled in the literature? Above I mentioned cycles, usually talked of as *booms* and *slumps*: but how might they be classified and effectively avoided?[15] And then there are the more obvious problems of the selling of half-finished goods or of the second-hand trade. But perhaps the one tricky puzzle that gets you homing in more seriously on the fundamental classification is the puzzle about, e.g., the new car-factory that is burnt down in the first week. The distinction between producer goods and consumer goods gets a jolt in that case, does it not? One thinks of a producer good as, say, in the relation of a point to a line: one factory, a flow of cars. How much flow is needed to be serious about this? Is this classification, then, way off?

In the next chapter I face, in subtle comic spirit, cousins of these questions. The tricky issue is that the questions are best faced when one actually has them prior to getting clues to their answer. There is a sense in which, it seems to me, as I struggle for my facing, us facing, you facing my invitation, there is something needed that is darkly prior to clues, clues that can be contaminated or disdained by a sick culture of meaning.

---

socialism, and his deep flaw is that he has no idea of the economic science that, e.g., the one-time Marxist Kalecki was searching for.

[14] My tossing around pointed to a big section of a possible introductory text, but it also led me to weave into chapter five a reflection on summary presentations.

[15] The classifications are given, in an elementary form, in *For a New Political Economy*, chapter 17, "Accelerations, Cycles, Phases." You might pause over the broad classifications given in the diagram at the bottom of page 274 there.

5

LOOSE ENDS

The original title to this chapter was "Indeterminacies," and that remains a central topic not unrelated to the new title, since "Loose Ends" certainly covers the curious looseness of the road to, and the terminal value of, a sane global economy.

First, though, I had best note simple indeterminacies of measurement that are intrinsic to economic analysis at its best. Perhaps a good start is to pause over a case of economic analysis at its worst. So I quote Joan Robinson in her best feistiness:

> The student of economic theory is taught to write $O = f(L, C)$ where L is a quantity of labour, C a quantity of capital and O a rate of output of commodities. He is instructed to assume all workers alike, and to measure L in man-hours of labour; he is told something about the index-number problem involved in choosing a unit of output; and then he is hurried on to the next question, in the hope that he will forget to ask in what units C is measured. Before ever he does ask, he has become a professor, and so sloppy habits of thought are handed on from one generation to the next.[1]

I see no point in entering, beyond my comment and footnoting, into the literature that confirms Robinson's bluntness, be it of her time or ours, of Capitalist or Marxist color. I quote rather a pedagogical piece from Bernard Lonergan on the subject of measurement, one that leaves us with precise problems regarding science—indeed, "the science of ethics" mentioned in the piece—that we only tackle in chapter twelve.

> It may help to clarify the issue if one distinguishes between normative, probable, and actual exchange values. One may say, 'A horse is worth two oxen,' and mean that a buyer *ought* to give me two oxen for my horse, when in point of fact he will give me no

---

[1] Joan Robinson, "The Production Function and the Theory of Capital," *Review of Economic Studies* vol. 21, no. 2 (1953–54), 81.

more than one. Again, one may say, 'A horse is worth two oxen,' and mean that I am *likely* to get two oxen for my horse if I attempt that exchange. The first of these statements is with regard to a *normative* exchange, and pertains to the science of ethics. The second of the statements is **about** a *probable* exchange value, and it pertains to the art of forecasting. But the exchange that concerns us is *actual* exchange value, and it emerges only subsequently to actual exchanges.[2]

Robinson and Lonergan share a common concern, the actual post-exchange exchange-value. Further, Lonergan has the more sophisticated perspective of the precise classifications breezed past in the previous chapter, and that perspective brings out more precisely the folly of various *a priori* theories of the exchange value of capital, labor, commodities. The magnificent piece of capital—or should I type *output*?—the *Titanic*, with commodities and labor on board, did not finish its first crossing of the Atlantic. What might theory say about a range of such products? The heuristics of classification pointed to in chapter four enables one to sort through the goings-on of financial backings and interests of global shipping possibilities, and distinguish classes of cargo, goods and service involved, resales, etc., etc. But Lonergan's heuristics is clear on the plethora of indeterminacies that keeps the science of such activities focused on actual exchanges.[3] Here we might well venture into concrete considerations of the varieties of indeterminacies, but that would muddle our little ramble with tasks of a long first-year text book. Still, you might well gain great light from pausing further over indeterminacies connected with such products as the *Titanic*, indeterminacies that spread their tentacles divergently: think of the *Titanic's* continued reach into memory, legend, cinema, research. But let us move along to consider—or should I write consider considering?—a general

---

[2] *For a New Political Economy*, 32. The view expressed is from his 1942 version of his analysis. The *about*, bold-faced above, is missing in the volume. Was this my editorial mistake or is it missing in Lonergan's typescript, which I no longer have? I would note the importance of this stand of Lonergan's for accuracy in measuring production: production includes sales. See *For a New Political Economy*, 114, 136, 247, 249. Revisit, now, Robinson's comment of the previous note, re measuring capital.

[3] We are following the same pointing as the previous two footnotes with their corresponding texts. On the related problem of "Economic Control," see the fragment of Lonergan's writing which I included, thus titled, in *For a New Political Economy*, 211–12.

This is exactly what Greenspan did not do!

indeterminacy: the relation between tons of steel and automobiles, between fishing trawlers and catches of fish, between air-miles and passenger-miles. I pause over the word *consider* and muse now over Bernard Lonergan's first paragraph of his four pages on our topic. His first three words, "the previous section," might be replaced now by you, in your musing, with "the previous chapter." Perhaps you noticed there the oddity in question here? Notice now the five words I bold-faced in my quotation below, which drove me, and now I hope you, to musing. Muse, for instance, over the eight words I add immediately here, "it is to be shown to present economists."

> The foregoing section isolated the productive process as a purely dynamic entity, and drew a distinction between consumer goods that enter the standard of living and producer goods that raise the standard of living. That distinction must now be examined more fully. **It is to be shown** that the correspondence between elements in the productive process and elements in the standard of living may be a point-to-point, or a point-to-line, or a point-to-surface, or even some higher correspondence.[4]

Occasionally I draw attention to the function of humor and satire. Here I can be humorous about my own efforts, my falling into what I now call the *short-trap*, a cousin of claptrap. My first view of this chapter was one that involved an aspiration to fulfill this dream or scream—do we not all spontaneously neuro-scream thus?—for fulfilling the inner demand of "it is to be shown."[5] Now, as I push on to a final version of the chapter I am

[4] *For a New Political Economy*, 234. The quotation is from his final analysis of 1944. There are four pages there on the point-to-point, etc., relations in the layers of the productive process. Did you hope they would be squeezed into a few lines here, when in fact what is needed is 5,000 words of colourful teaching talk? Muse over the next note. Think of it personally; think of it ontically and phyletically; think if it as in the tension of arias and poems and nocturnes.

[5] This is a deep human demand and aspiration, one I would have you think of in relation to the various shows like *America's Got Talent*. One can think of it also in terms of talented people like those two who died at age 27: Amy Winehouse and Kurt Cobain. But here I raise the issue more prosaically, yet about this whole little performance of mine. I wrote, 30 years ago, "As I grow older I believe less and less in summary expression, even when one has reached a worthwhile perspective. Too many people seem willing to attempt for Lonergan what Fichte attempted for Kant, or what De Quincey attempted for Ricardo. I have little faith in such attempts, particularly if they have no content driving rhythmically from below upwards towards morning dreams and images." "Systematics, Communications,

tempted to squeeze a summary into footnote 5: which I resist doing. The telling indeed might be a success in the four-volume work I mentioned at the end of the Introduction. In a sense to be hinted at in chapter thirteen, we have not got the nerve, in our axial times, for genuine human communication. This perhaps is summed up nicely—LOL: summary again!—in the tradition of the publication *Scientific American*. Some of us battle our way to getting a grip on the meaning of the Higgs particle, but the majority in our axial warp-speed want Higgs served up for breakfast. The presentation that I had initially hoped to communicate here of indeterminacies of point-to-line etc., relations would have been a summary of four pages:[6] who was I kidding? And in what way am I just kidding around, kidding me, kidding you, when I think of the meaning of "squeezing into a note 5" here?

Am I kidding around right through the book? In a sense, yes. So, I could not expect the busy businessman Donald Trump to even begin to tackle chapter two seriously, much less climb to a view of the axial blindness regarding profit and regarding climbing, climbing to make America really great. Later[7] we shall summarily seize—LOL—what I do realistically expect. But here I wish to stir your nerves to imagine two loose ends that are intimately related.

Perhaps it is useful, if not best, to start with the stuttering appeal, in 2000, of Will Steffen, executive director then of the International Geosphere-Biosphere Program: "Stop using the word *Holocene*. We're not in the Holocene any more. We're in the . . . the . . . the . . . the Anthropocene!"[8] He was commenting on research reports about that Holocene period of the past 12,000 years, on which he was reflecting in his "An Integrated Approach to Understanding Earth's Metabolism."

The emergence of the new Anthropocene focus is well documented in Ian Angus' new book, and it is to that book that I now turn to bring to your

---

Actual Contexts," *Lonergan Workshop*, ed. Fred Lawrence, vol. 6 (Atlanta, GA: Scholars Press, 1986), 147. I am much clearer now on the missing neuromolecular dynamics of present cultures: we shall pause over it in chapter thirteen. A background to this entire issue is Robert Henman, *Global Collaboration: Neuroscience as Paradigmatic* (Vancouver: Axial Publishing, 2016).

[6] The four pages already mentioned in note 4: *For a New Political Economy*, 234–237.

[7] See especially chapter fifteen below. That, I hope will further stir your nerves. But if you are a journalist, let your nerves be stirred by the idea of a Pullet's Surprise.

[8] *The Future of Nature* (New Haven: Yale University Press, 2013), 486.

attention the key loose end to which I must attend in Part Three. He asks, "When did the Anthropocene begin?" and he focuses eloquently on what I call *the Negative Anthropocene*. He is, in a sense, a new Marx writing of the end of capitalism, but his offer is of a new socialism. Rightly he is looking for "A Second Copernican Revolution,"[9] and he sweeps magnificently through the story of the idiocies, the stupidities and the cupidities, of the industrial revolution. But the effort fizzles out in his final chapter, "The Movement We Need." It is a little like Jesus trying out the Beatitudes on the Hebrew crowd.[10] He continues—am I talking here about Angus or Jesus?—a long tradition of tossing round initial meanings in a rich relational fashion without a pause regarding Anthropos.[11] But I had best leave talk of that for later. My main point regarding Angus' effort is that we are not at the end of capitalism: we are at the end of the road regarding economic nonsense. The new road starts in chapter two above.

I turn finally here to the other loose end, one that relates to the failure of Angus's final chapter. Again, LOL at summary pointing.[12] My interest is in what might be considered the failed last chapter of Bernard Lonergan's book on the Copernican revolution.[13] He writes there of a final stage of the cycles of the revolution in which "reflection bears fruit."[14] The reality of that

---

[9] The title of his first chapter.

[10] I raise a massively complex question here about the non-scientific character of ancient wisdom and of the biblical studies that hover over such wisdom, something to be mused over creatively in this next millennium. Best for now just to throw the question into another interesting context. Brendan Lovett writes: "In the midst of modern crises of cultural transition in China there was a Jesuit appeal to the ethos of the beatitudes. The Sermon on the Mount must have sounded like romantic escapism. 'Is that all you have to offer us?' incredulous Chinese intellectuals asked the sons of Matteo Ricci." *A Dragon not for the Killing* (Quezon City: Claretian Press, 1998), at note 13 of chapter 2, "Ambiguities in Cultural Transformation."

[11] I think here also of the linguistics periodical *Anthropos*, which has been doing, for over a century, what I accuse Angus of doing. In my *A Brief History of Tongue: From Big Bang to Coloured Wholes* (Halifax: Axial Publications, 1998) I introduce in chapter one the anthropos Helen Keller and her leap to language. The *Anthropos* writers have managed to cover a great deal about language in decades of increasing subtlety without meeting either Helen or their whatting selves.

[12] Read now, freshly, note 13 of the previous chapter.

[13] I am referring to the fourteenth chapter of *Method in Theology*, titled "Communications." I have dealt with it in some detail in my *The Allure of the Compelling Genius of History*, 187–221.

[14] Lonergan, *Method in Theology*, 355.

fruit is that it is to be a cyclically-effective education, something we shall grapple with in chapter twelve below. Or shall we? Can you get beyond my dark twisting and its seeming avoidance of convenient clarities? What is this weaving doing? It "primarily is pedagogical: it is headed towards an end that is unknown and as yet cannot be disclosed; from the viewpoint of the pupil, it proceeds by cajoling or forcing attention and not by explaining the intended goal and by inviting an intelligent and reasonable cooperation."[15]

And here I halt, with so many loose ends left about loose ends. So, have we not, here within us and between us, perhaps impatient or even angry optic nerves, molecularly locked in the wish to move comfortably in straight lines of accumulated accessible meaning? It is, in you now, something of the tension of a nocturne entrancingly heard, or might it be the tense irritation of a night in shining industrial armor?[16]

---

[15] Lonergan, *Insight*, 423.

[16] I cannot resist a final strange aside about non-summary. I attempted, in one of my series, to share something of my search for the meaning of a single page of a work of Lonergan: *Insight*, 489, "study of an organism begins . . ." My commentary grew into 41 essays titled "Field Nocturnes." What, then, of you, organism, reaching for a neuromolecular grip on "the very pulse of the machine"? *For a New Political Economy*, 326. See note 8 of the following chapter, page 33 below. There is the comic aspect of trying to initiate a shift from a well-settled global erroneous drifting to a positive Anthropocene climb in the cosmos!

6

PROFIT I

When I had finished indexing the book that is at the heart of finding the meaning of profit—Lonergan's *For a New Political Economy*—it was sufficiently clear to me that central to this hearty meaning was the largest entry in the index, that which is under the word *Concomitance*.[1] I wrote a short introduction to the index which concluded with a quotation from a poem of Wordsworth: "And now I see with eye serene / The very pulse of the machine."[2] There is a remote meaning of profit and its uses that weaves its simpler identification in *concomitances* into the body politic as measures of pulse and blood-pressure weave into the healthy rhythms of the human body. How well did I serenely see that remote meaning in 1998? Later chapters, such as that on "International Credit,"[3] show my struggle forward, but an immediate learned footnote reveals how I serenely missed the connection to *Concomitance* and the concomitance of Mark Blaug's question, "Why is the quantity theory of money the oldest surviving theory of economics?"[4]

Yet there is a deeper issue that asks simply for a theory of money, and foggy theories survive all the way from views of primitive exchanges to

---

[1] *For a New Political Economy*, 329. It is surely obvious that I cannot communicate the meaning of **concomitance** here or in this little book. The third last paragraph of this chapter is one that is an "elementary musing," but lurking there is the full concrete issue of concomitance, of Marx and Keynes, of quarterly profits and living wage. The real issue is that some of you readers who notice the "obvious" will effectively promote the beginning of a climb to a startlingly different world economy.

[2] *Ibid.*, 326.

[3] Chapter seven below, 39–46.

[4] This is chapter 2 of Mark Blaug et al., *The Quantity Theory of Money from Locke to Keynes and Friedman* (Brookfield, VT: Edward Elgar Publishers, 1995). For the solution to the quantity theory problem see my Appendix, "Trade Turnover and the Quantity Theory of Money" either to Philip McShane, *Pastkeynes Pastmodern Economics*, 137–53, or to Bruce Anderson and Philip McShane, *Beyond Establishment Economics: No Thank You, Mankiw*, 237–54.

arrogance about the creative value of commodity money[5] and, reaching way beyond that, to an optimism about the disappearance of money. That reaching beyond is worth quoting at this early stage in our musing about profit, in that it raises strange imaginings about the story of the sweep—or should I say the sweeping away?—of America's landscape.

Nor is it impossible that further developments in science should make small units self-sufficient on an ultramodern standard of living to eliminate commerce and industry, to transform agriculture into a superchemistry, to clear away finance and even money, to make economic solidarity a memory, and power over nature the only difference between high civilization and primitive gardening.[6]

Nudged imaginatively by this ranging round, we can now venture better towards facing in a most elementary form, the question, "What is profit?" So, we carry forward our simpler reflections of chapter two on there being two types of firm and chapter three's elementary illustration of innovation as effecting monetary flows around those two types of firm. A parallel with the study of hydrodynamics helps here. What is water motion? I think of an old friend and colleague, Patrick Crean, studying the wave-motions between Vancouver and Vancouver Island: a life's work.[7] Here we poise over profit and its waves in parallel with simple pulsing experiments in a swimming pool.

---

[5] This is a tricky zone, but here think simply, however vaguely, of the strategies described in Ron Suskind's *Confidence Men* (see note 17 on page v): the "banking industry, which over the past couple of decades has grown vast and insatiable by inventing, for the most part, new ways to market, sell, and invest debt." Connect this with the normative economics that, already stressed by complexities of indeterminacies (see the lengthy quotation at note 119 in Chapter Seven, and note 96 below), must rise to a clean-up of the gangsterisms and the sicknesses that haunt what Lonergan calls *the redistribution function.*

[6] *For a New Political Economy*, 20. That quotation is continued on pages 102–103, below.

[7] See P.B. Crean, T.S. Murty, and J.A. Stronach, *Lecture Notes on Coastal and Estuarine Studies* (New York, Springer-Verlag, 1988). This volume is one of thirty volumes with this general title. The volume is subtitled *Mathematical Modelling of Tidal and Estuarine Circulation: The Coastal Seas of Southern British Columbia and Washington State.* For further pointers re the parallel between Hydrodynamics and Economic Dynamics see Chapter 4, "Do You Want a Sane Global Economics?" of my *Sane Economics and Fusionism*, pp. 41–54 and notes 116, 117, on page 103.

What we have to get to grips with, as quite natural or mechanical in any venture of innovation in the process, be it simple or massively complex, is the fundamental rhythmic pattern of the two flows of goods and a *concomitant* patterning of purchasings. The stationary state may be imaged as the pool at rest, even though this imagining covers up that the economic stationary state is intrinsically dynamic. The final state, from a particular type of nudging in the pool's water, is a steady state of standing waves. But what lies in between? That is the object of tricky analysis in the shockingly simple water-wave illustration. You would do well to envisage that illustration in detail. Think of the business of tooling up, of investing in a pool-width plank to start the disturbance, of collaborating to get the oscillating properly underway. Investing in the plank and other needed elements have, of course, monetary aspects that can push you to think differently of parallels in the economic shift that is our interest.[8] Imagination needs to stretch to think perhaps of the innovation of a new global game, a Pokémon of pools. One group may have the advantage of being the original innovators, but soon other groups get in on the innovation and add twists of personal talents. Thus you find yourself paralleling the world of Joseph Schumpeter's analysis of the sequential dynamics of innovation, its spread, and its lags.

But the present existential crisis is in the here-now question: "Am I up to or for this pause over details, up to taking at least a month off to meet history's challenge?"

If you are, then, after that month or some dozens of months you may well write these next two paragraphs, smiling through your citing of

---

Might you pause here and muse over what the equivalent of the IMF or the World Bank would be, and do, in this global world of small rhythms?

[8] A central comic pause is needed over this sentence. I recall a letter of James Joyce answering a query. After a few pages of hints and suggestions he ended, "if I can throw any further obscurity on the matter let me know." I deliberately began the sentence in the text with the word *investing* and ended it with the word *interest*. Yet I was, and have been in chapters four, five, and six, pushing you, by twists of obscurity, to think away from conventional meanings of these words, monetary aspects of economic dynamics that distract from the needed economic analysis. The most famous instance of such distraction is John Hick's simplistic focus on interest—in the financial sense—in 1937 which turned Keynes' effort of 1936 into a simpler business of jollying along with IS/LM curves. (On debates around the IS/LM muddlings, see my *Pastkeynes Pastmodern Economics*, 65–69). The distraction I have been avoiding here, since chapter three, is the simplistic focus on bogus clarity: think, now, of your probably mounting frustration as you wait for what is not coming in this chapter: a neat new definition of profit.

Chesterton's quip as you flow on from the existential now that follows the work, a written now that recalls the perhaps month-long now of the starting sentence, "**Now** I have been looking at the dynamic structure of the industrial exchange economy." And I smile here after giving this twist to my text, knowing that after fifty years I have poised you properly and discomfortingly over the block to this massive cultural transformation. Did you really expect to get my point over an Einsteinian cup of tea?![9]

After you have been thus looking, then you may write the next two paragraphs. If you have done your home-working, you will luminously note and cherish how much of chapters two to five haunt your thinking of the increasing and decreasing of money-in-hand for boosting standards of production or standards of daily benefittings, and when you re-read it later, with chapters seven to ten under your pelt, you will wonder at the glory of it all, and when you, as butterflying from the end of the book, return to read again our possessed and possessing two paragraphs, you will exult in the glory as only a beginning.

> Now I have been looking at the dynamic structure of the industrial exchange economy. In it I have distinguished stationary states, increasing returns that arise when the economy is tooling up for increased production but as yet not thereby increasing living standards, and the decreasing returns that arise for investors when tooling up is tapering off and the flow of consumer goods and services is increasing.

> I beg to note that such an analysis has not been tried and found wanting. Rather, to speak with Chesterton, it has been thought hard and not tried.[10] What has been tried is roughly as follows: (1) the emergence of industrial nations as creditors and others as debtors, (2) the establishment of colonies and empires, their rivalries and wars, (3) the rise of the arch-secularist Marx, the industrial development of the U.S.S.R., its diplomatic and warlike achievements, and the moral support it enjoys from secularists elsewhere, (4) the welfare state with its substitutes for a properly functioning basic phase and with its crumbling foundations in

---

[9] See above, 3–4, and think of our pause over the problem of summarizing in chapter five.

[10] "The Christian ideal has not been tried and found wanting. It has been found difficult and left untried." G.K. Chesterton, *What's Wrong with the World* (New York: Sheed & Ward, 1956), 29 (in "The Unfinished Temple," 27–32).

economic science, and (5) the multinational corporations, their flourishing but offshore economy, and the dual economies[11] they effect not only in the underdeveloped countries but also in the United States.[12]

Have these two dense paragraphs given you pause? It would be an amazing given shriven pause if you Now turned aside, built a Now-bow-wow around your daze to let your psyche be seized by the slimly revealed existential gap in your inherited molecularly-fixed view of economic goings-on—whether or not you have the standard education in standard economics or not. Most likely by far there is a tendency to move on, to see perhaps what Part Two might offer to ease the obscurity. One way or another it seems best for me to move on, cycle round, in chapters seven and eight, an international version of chapters two and three. Then, after we pause again—what sort of pause, you may ask?—over the original and originating climb of the man who wrote the first sentence of the quotation at note 12, and ask freshly, "What is profit?"

But meantime a little elementary musing helps. Think back to the island and the invention of the plough. Who profits? Obviously the island community profits. It was a promise fermented forward by a tavern chat, a promise involving promissory notes of various types naming and fixing a loose integration of aggregates of promises and activities. The realization of the promises involved rhythms, and the better heuristically understood the rhythms, the neater could the promises "go with the flow." Did the prime initiator of the innovation profit, beyond the satisfaction of the achievement, in a lift of living-standard meshed with a possession of notes of promise?[13]

---

[11] A long editors' note here comments on various aspects of the phenomena discussed by Richard Barnet and Ronald Müller in *Global Reach: The Power of the Multinational Corporations* (New York, Simon & Schuster, 1974). This early phenomenology needs to be lifted into a richer later literature and meshed into considerations of the madness of the financial shenanigans instituted in the years since.

[12] Lonergan, *Macroeconomic Dynamics*, 95–96. This was a 1982 addition to his work of the early 1940s.

[13] Promise? I would note that there is nothing fuzzy, foolish, or fanciful about the promise pointed to in this paragraph or in this little book. I am pointing to a science of economics that promises a deep shift of income distribution, leaping beyond Marx's gallant muddles, beyond the ungallant voodoo of present political economics, beyond the gallivanting of Piketty through history. It is quite beyond the comprehension of those who con-descend to talk of little lifts in minimum

That would be taken for granted by the community, as well as a range of income-flows that somehow were both a sane measure of contributions to the realization of the promise and a nudge towards further innovations and promises, stepping stones to a promised land for children and grandchildren. Might one speak of a promised land the world over? Might one ask if somehow Joey's entire island profits from the rhythms of innovation? In what way might there be some element of the free-flowing and the global-flying in the full meaning of profit, the rhythmic inclusion of a sort of pure wild-card surplus?

So I end this first chapter on Profit in an elementary musing that is, is it not, amazingly simple and familiar, indeed, in some sense, "true but obvious and insignificant."[14] Yet, in the fullness of its presuppositions, it is massively strange to the world over. And it is in quite a different world of realistic long-term aspirations from the monodisciplinary descriptive puttering of Mervyn King's eighth chapter, "Healing and Hubris: The World Economy Today."[15] That different world meshes with the interdisciplinary world reached for by Lonergan in "Healing and Creating in History." Why not end here as he ended that essay?

> Is my proposal utopian? It asks merely for creativity, for an interdisciplinary theory that at first will be denounced as absurd, then will be admitted to be true but obvious and insignificant, and perhaps finally be regarded as so important that its adversaries will claim that they themselves discovered it.[16]

---

wages. But the shift demands an initial revolution in economic departments, especially in the elementary courses trapped in silly non-empirical pseudo-science. The possibility of President Trump starting the revolution is touched on here and there in my little book but it is surely clear enough now that the challenge involves the public and its journalists becoming effectively articulate: starting, of course, with you. We really have had enough of highly-paid economic and political witch-doctors, have we not?

[14] See the quotation that ends the chapter.

[15] See note 7 on page 20 above.

[16] Lonergan, concluding an essay titled "Healing and Creating in History," reprinted in his *Macroeconomic Dynamics, CWL* 15, 106.

PART TWO

BROADER GROUNDS

7

IMAGING INTERNATIONAL CREDIT

It seems best to include immediately the original summary of the project, since it helps us to see the reach of our search and the need for a limited expression of it in this short presentation. We are reaching for a helpful heuristic imaging that is empirically rich and historical. Here, then, is the original summary context.

Between 1942 and 1944 Lonergan moved to an imaging of international economics which enabled him to begin controlling its meaning heuristically. There remained problems for him, such as "The Financial Problem" with which he concluded the 1942 typescript. He concludes that section, and the typescript, by noting that "it is a vast task. It means thinking out afresh our ideas of markets, prices, international trade, investment, return on capital."[1] I wish to bring *Insight*'s frontispiece from Aristotle and the fundamental thesis of the book to bear on this task. The Club of Rome made popular the slogan "think globally, act locally." The Aristotelian twist to be given this is "Image globally and locally," and the imaging is to be proleptic. I wish to place Lonergan's enabling imaging of international circulation as through the redistribution function[2] in a larger context of a global imaging of two surface spheres of micro-oscillations. To that imaging there is to be added a functional imaging that brings economics and ecology into a symbiotic dynamics. The result will relate heuristically to a sublation of both ecological movements and global struggles with monetary bailouts into a grounding proleptic imaging of "all the concrete inventiveness, all the capacity for discovery and for adaptation, that we can command."[3]

The historical context I have in mind can be connected immediately with the final quotation of the summary, and indeed it can be represented, imaged, by a recent book: *The International Organization of Credit*.[4] I would note

---

[1] *For a New Political Economy. CW 21*, 105. I refer to this work below as **FNPE**.

[2] **FNPE**, 309.

[3] **FNPE**, 105–6.

[4] Randall D. Germain, *The International Organization of Credit: States and Global Finance in the World-Economy* (Cambridge: Cambridge University Press, 1997), to be referred

immediately, and importantly, that we are now on topic, the topic of imaging, and it alerts my present audience both to the problem of the relevant audience, and to the present audience's possible problem of an existential gap.[5]

The problem of the relevant audience is that the relevant audience is absent, or might join us only by slim chance, and further, that this joining would be problematic at best, radically uncomprehending at worst. That relevant audience is the community engaged in studying and operating international credit. Why would their joining, if it occurred, be problematic or uncomprehending? Because the norm implicit in our inquiry is the norm set out so clearly by Lonergan regarding generalized empirical method.

> Generalized empirical method operates on a combination of both the data of sense and the data of consciousness: it does not treat of objects without taking into account the corresponding operations of the subject; it does not treat of the subject's operations without taking into account the corresponding objects.[6]

This norm is incomprehensible to the present culture of either economic studies or economic practice. Certainly the groups mentioned use the language of economic decisions, but it is a language cut off by psychic truncation from anything but truncated meaning.

Nor is this short presentation the place to spell this out: it is a massive problem of our axial time, one that, paradoxically, takes on meaning for us as present audience only if that same norm of generalized empirical method is taken seriously by us, if only proleptically, in an incarnate intussusception of the problem of the existential gap.

Here we must return to the discomforting message of *Insight*. The norm of generalized empirical method "is a rule of extreme importance, for the failure to observe it results in the substitution of a pseudo-metaphysical mythmaking for scientific inquiry."[7] We can all too easily, out of our rich common sense, talk of international credit and banking in a cultured fashion and with "an air of profundity."[8] But that is not the scientific inquiry

---

to below as **IOC**. It is one of many that would serve our purpose, but more recommendable than most.

[5] See Lonergan, *CW18*, index, on *Existential Gap*.

[6] Lonergan, *A Third Collection*, 141.

[7] *Insight*, 528.

[8] *Ibid.*, 566.

warranted by the present century's problems of finance. Witness the talk of the present community of operators in America in the area of credit, all the way from the freneticism of Wall Street to the poise of the White House. The existential gap is a present cruel reality and it is "through this gap that there proudly march the speculative gnostic and the practical magician."[9] Our challenge, the challenge of this audience, is to be luminous regarding that gap in us, if it exists. What is this problem of international credit and its imaging? The small handful **IOC** is an image, or even smaller the two-page image of its Appendix. That Appendix names five centuries of top banks in a sequence of centres beginning with Antwerp in the sixteenth century and inviting us to meet the operators of Amsterdam, London, Berlin, and New York. We reach back to Fugger and on to the Lehman Brothers and beyond. Or do we; or can we?[10]

But now I must add the key image that I would suggest as dominating the immediate effort to glimpse the real problem of twenty-first century credit. It is an image that fits beautifully with the drive of IOC through history, but first envisage it ahistorically. The image in question, in our questing eye and kinesthetic sensibility, is the image mentioned in the summary above: an image of two surface spheres of micro-oscillations covering the globe. In its most elementary form it is a two-dimensional drawing of three close circles, the two outermost being slightly irregular. Think of the inner circle as the surface of the earth, taken as uniform and watery. Then the next circle can be imagined as like the ups and downs of the ocean's flows. But why the second such image of ocean flows? Because we are imaging the actualities of any economy that we know of: two layers of flow, production goods and consumer goods. And that imaging, in its simplicity, is to be placed in the context of the global village's challenge to

---

[9] *Ibid.*, 565.

[10] **IOC** and the listing of banks only represents the edge of the problem of global finance as it shifts from banking to other structures. *Financialization and the World Economy*, edited by Gerald A. Epstein (Northampton, MA: Edward Elgar, 2005), adds a context. "One key characteristic of the global financial system is now widely recognized to be its complexity and obscurity, which few are able to penetrate." *Global Finance in the New Century: Beyond Deregulation*, ed. Libby Assassi, Anastasia Nesvetailova and Duncan Wigan (Hampshire: Palgrave Macmillan, 2007), page 1 of the editors' introductory article. I highly recommend the article in relation to its unknowing attention to the contemporary mediated blocking of concomitance: see the next note. The penetration involves a slow education (see *CW* 15, 119) into the heuristics sketched briefly here, with its new norms of success (again, see the following note) and of explanatory and functional global care.

meet the promise of money: a concomitance[11] of the two flows, within the dynamics of our feeble human creativities, which would gently lift our standard of pilgrim living to new unimaginable levels of love and leisure.[12]

Nor is it impossible that further developments in science should make small units self-sufficient on an ultra-modern standard of living to eliminate commerce and industry, to transform agriculture into a superchemistry, to clear away finance and even money, to make economic solidarity a memory, and power over nature the only difference between high civilization and primitive gardening. But we are not there yet.[13]

But how do we get there, how do we gently lift?

Before moving to that question in summary fashion, I wish to complement the global diagram with the second half of a fragment Lonergan wrote on "Economic Control" that I included in pages 211–12 of *For a New Political Economy*. He refers to the simple diagram, the baseball diagram that is familiar from the 1944 analysis.

Evidently, there is a high degree of indeterminacy to events within such a dynamic structure. All one can say is the game may go all awry. A large and positive crossover difference uncompensated by action from the pitcher's box will result sooner or later in depriving the groups at second and third bases of all their balls, or if the crossover difference is large and negative, it will result in depriving the groups at home and first of all their balls. Similarly if the group at the pitcher's box makes up its mind to accumulate balls, tossing fewer than they receive, the groups at the bases will again find themselves without balls eventually. But without further information one cannot say how rapidly the ultimate event of being without balls will arrive. Further, the players at the bases may make up, by a greater efficiency in pitching and catching what

---

[11] The word *concomitance* symbolizes the full challenge, a point I made in the introduction to the index of *CW* 21. Its incarnation in the global community of business is to give a strange salvific meaning to *success*, massively different from profit-seeking.

[12] Lurking in Lonergan's view is an orientation to leisure within human history, and a theory of dis-employment. See **FNPE**, 18–20, 22, 25, 189.

[13] *For a New Political Economy*, 20.

balls they have, for any loss of balls they might suffer, up to the ultimate moment when they have no balls at all.

But despite this almost baffling indeterminacy, it remains that there is a definite dynamic structure. There are hypotheses on which the game can go awry; and this possibility constitutes a fundamental indeterminacy for the structure. On that basis either by adding further information about the nature of the game or by adding further suppositions, a still greater determinacy may be built.[14]

Paradoxically, adding the global diagram, with new layers of indeterminacy, is such an additional determinacy.[15]

When presenting the image I asked that it be viewed initially in an ahistorical fashion. Strictly, of course, this is not possible: one needs to imagine a slice of history that enables the inclusion of rhythms. But if one is reaching for a diagram that holds together, say, the topic of four centuries, as IOC does, then one is in a world of Markov matrix thinking,[16] but now imaged with the timeline originating at the center of the sphere that represents the earth. Nor is the imaging some isolation of economic rhythms: the imaging is to be a fusion, without confusion, of other events and rhythms. The imaging, indeed, is to be, eventually, the framework for a geohistorical genetic systematics, an ongoing freshened fractal framework of the cyclic control of human meaning that includes a geohistorical grip on all types of doctrinal contexts.[17]

Do I go too far here with the oddities of the task of imaging? I do not, indeed, nor cannot here, go far enough: for the imaging is an eschatological

---

[14] **FNPE**, 211–212.

[15] There is a massive problem here of human minding that relates to the absence of a grip on the place of primary and secondary determinations of finite forms in that minding. It affects all areas, starting with the simple science of physics' mythic overreachings for unifications. Here it is a matter of centralist sillinesses in a world of stupidity, malice, and wars. Minding has to struggle towards a new luminosity of the emergent probabilities that haunt local events.

[16] See Philip McShane, *Randomness, Statistics and Emergence* (London and South Bend IN: Gill, Macmillan and Notre Dame, 1970), 237.

[17] The compact statement is opaque without such an effort as is invited by the pointers in *Prehumous* 2 (available at: http://www.philipmcshane.org/prehumous), or (more fully) *Method in Theology: Revisions and Implementations* (available at: http://www.philipmcshane.org/website-books). In particular, I must leave to the reader the task of meshing in ecological searchings.

and everlasting human task. But let us stick with pilgrim meaning, with the anticipation of a maturing of pilgrim metaphysics. I return to Lonergan's best description of that pilgrim task.

This comprehending of everything in a unified whole can be either formal or virtual. It is virtual when one is habitually able to answer readily and without difficulty, or at least 'without tears,' a whole series of questions right up to the last 'why?' Formal comprehension, however, cannot take place without a turning to phantasm; but in larger and more complex questions it is impossible to have a suitable phantasm unless the imagination is aided by some sort of diagram. Thus, if we want a comprehensive grasp of everything in a unified whole, we shall have to construct a diagram in which are symbolically represented all the various elements of the question along with all the connections between them.[18]

There is here a lead to a multilayered "symbolic indication of the total range of possible experience"[19] needed for an effective metaphysics. It points to a deep sense of *general* and *generalization* that I have written of previously, a sense that would distract us into larger expression and strange hopes, indeed, of the generalization that is a sublating mesh of *Insight* and *Method in Theology*.[20] I may well cut to the chase in my reaching for both a generalization of *Method in Theology* and a method of generalizing by turning to the final section of chapter one of *For a New Political Economy*.

First, let us pause, "descend to familiar things." The familiar things are the events surrounding the bailout efforts of the present American government. How are we, they, to bail out a boat awash in a century of stupidity and cupidity? Only very slowly, and with century-long patience, on a layered[21] set of massively skewed baseball diamonds. But what is needed for that is a new Standard Model of human collaboration, a new general

---

[18] Lonergan, *The Ontological and Psychological Constitution of Christ*, vol. 7, *Collected Works of Bernard Lonergan* (Toronto: University of Toronto Press, 2002), 151.

[19] *Insight* 396.

[20] I can only hint here at a fresh meaning of *general* as rooted in a **generative** luminosity of *notio entis* to oneself in the personal sublation of *Insight*'s and *Method*'s searching pointers towards an empirically-rich and implementable general heuristics.

[21] "Like old-style records, with each circuit diagram linked with others through a central funnel." McShane, *Economics for Everyone*, 108.

metaphysics. So, let us venture into that two-page section of **FNPE**, chapter one, by savoring the first paragraph.

> The method of generalization cannot be judged by previous standards. On the contrary, unless there is a notable divergence, one can be certain that there is no generalization. This should be clear from what has been said already, but it will be no harm to reinforce the point, for the inertia coefficient of the human mind is normally rather high.[22]

Witness, indeed, that inertia's destructive presence in the familiar things of Lonerganism's writings that take no account of the notable divergence of *Method's* definition of general and special metaphysics from the ineffective definition of *Insight*.

I descend, discomfortingly, to familiar things, papers and conferences and talk of progress that are cast in an old stale effete mode. And I must ask you to take seriously the third paragraph of that section.

> Despite the fact that the argument is supposed to be a generalization, still at times it does descend to familiar things. There is no fault in that, for one cannot live in thin air. But there does appear to be this fault, that such descents to the concrete, insofar as they use familiar terms, do so in quite unfamiliar fashion.[23]

The descent, within the Tower of Able that is to emerge in the 22nd century, is to be from a communally embraced and embracing comeabout[24] perspective, lifted existentially to invisible fusion by the intussusception of the canons of hermeneutics, all "being fused into a single explanation,"[25] meshed with its genetically-fermenting framework of imaging. The meshing calls "not merely for sober and balanced speculation but also for all the concrete inventiveness, all the capacity for discovery and adaptation, that we

---

[22] **FNPE**, 8.
[23] **FNPE**, 8.
[24] The comeabout perspective is that given in the sentence of *Insight* 514 [537] that begins, "So it comes about ...."
[25] *Insight* 587.

can command,"[26] solving "the problem of general history, which is the real catch."[27] "Plainly the way out is through the more general field."[28]

If here we have insisted on the importance of generalization, that is only because generalization is our undertaking. We would not be thought to make little of the complementary element of science, the solid stimulus and saving control of fact. On the contrary, it is only to give account of enormous facts overlooked by political economy and by specialized economics that this generalization is undertaken, and it is only by a new study of facts, more fully grasped because more broadly seen, that our general conclusions can be made a source of practical applications.[29]

The new practical study of cosmic facts, a distant fantasy, is to bud forth from a functional cyclic collaboration sustained by neuromolecules' surges of imagings that gives international credit to God.

---

[26] **FNPE**, 105–106.

[27] Lonergan, *Topics in Education*, 236. On the solution to the problem of general history in terms of functionality, see *Field Nocturnes CanTower* 50, "*Insight* Within a New Global Culture" (available at: http://www.philipmcshane.org/field-nocturnes-cantower), a paper from the Australian Lonergan Conference of 2007. The conference papers are available in *Fifty Years of* Insight: *Bernard Lonergan's Contribution to Philosophy and Theology*, ed. Neil Ormerod et al. (Adelaide: Australian Theological Forum Press, 2011).

[28] **FNPE**, 7. I would have you lift, by strenuous fantasy, these reaches of 1942 into the context of Lonergan's later reflections on **The Field**: see *CWL* 18, index, under *Field*.

[29] **FNPE**, 10.

8

GOVERNMENT & GLOBE

The present topic is probably the most manifest to you, even if you are only a beginner in economics. Government taxation clutches at your earning and spending. The media tune you into trade agreements and third world debts. Yet to get beyond the manifest to what is the heart of the matter and the mess is not easy. Economics journals are contemporarily cluttered with erudite articles on taxation structures, fluctuations of exchange rates, export policies of less developed countries, and the international debt problem. Our introductory efforts here cannot reach into these subtleties, but perhaps by the end of some serious work on this chapter you will have an angle, the beginnings of a perspective, on missing components of contemporary searchings in the economics of international trade and government operations.

You already have a line on what is missing through your elementary glimpse of the two flows in the economy brought together by our basic diagramming of flows and crossovers. Present economics does not have, much less grow round, these distinctions. The basic and surplus circuits and the requirements for their balanced twining are not a topic in first year university texts, and the absence carries the students forward into the staleness, disorientation, and relative irrelevance of present economic theorizing and advising on trading and taxing. So what we add here to the view of the previous chapters will not resemble regular treatments of these topics. To the precision of our diagram of circuits we will add, superpose, circuits that correspond to operations of international trade and national government. But further, to deal with international economics, we must add diagram to diagram, where each diagram corresponds to what is accepted as an economic unit, a nation or group of nations.[1] Bernard Lonergan, in his first effort to handle this topic, wrote:

---

[1] Jane Jacobs, *Cities and the Wealth of Nations* (New York: Random House, 1984), is helpful here on the problem of economic units and local autonomies. Also useful is Joan Robinson and John Eatwell, *An Introduction to Modern Economics* (New York:

Whether from mental fatigue or from objective impossibility, I do not see that a general study of the interactions of several mechanical structures is possible. The problems are far too complex. However, what is possible is the solution of particular issues. Then a definite and limited objective is assigned the inquirer, and as these issues arise he can prescind from an infinity of irrelevancies to track down the precise point at hand.[2]

We have a limited objective here: to track down in a broad manner the effects of trade and government on the rhythms of the two circuits. The key to the necessary enlargement of our discussion, of getting beyond considerations of a closed economy, is to link economies through their redistributive functions. It may help, initially, to imagine our island thus linked up to the rest of the globe as a unit: so you will have two diagrams of circuits. If your imagination is up to it you can go further to link the world's economic units in layers, like old-style records, with each circuit diagram linked with others only through a central funnel.

Let us venture into the topic of a favorable balance of foreign trade in surplus goods and services. We will consider it to be a steady flow, of the same character as the other flows in our diagram: let us say, Z'' per interval. To reach for the fundamental insights here we slide past concrete complications of exchange rates, lags, multipliers, whatever. I must appeal to you, especially to professional economists, to tolerate this sliding. For instance, my considerations of government operations could well call up questions like, 'What of the balanced-budget multiplier?' Such questions are legitimate advanced questions. We are in the foothills, and this is perhaps best brought out by our sticking with simple extensions of the illustrations from chapter one of *Economics for Everyone*. So here think of ploughs as being the export surplus good from our island. It will not be too difficult for you, later, to shift to the problem of the export of agribusiness capital goods from that small island off the coast of China, North America, to less developed islands.[3]

McGraw Hill, 1973) on the question "Why is there a problem of the balance of payments for the UK but not for the county of Oxfordshire?" *Ibid.*, 245.

[2] **FNPE**, 94. It was nor, of course, a matter of fatigue: economic process is multiply non-systematic. See Lonergan, *Insight*, the index under *non-systematic*.

[3] "The habitable dry land surface of the biosphere consists of a single continent, Asia, together with its peninsulas and off-shore islands ... the three largest of Asia's off-shore islands are Africa and the two Americas." Arnold Toynbee, *Mankind and Mother Earth* (Oxford: Oxford University Press, 1976), 32.

The ploughs, obviously, are purchased by exporters. For a start think of these exporters as availing somehow of the redistribution function to add to surplus demand. The availing somehow may seem mysterious to you. Think of it as a problem to be dealt with in a second-year university course in finance. It is a matter of financial market operations in short-term loans or long-terms securities regarding the establishment of a foreign debt or the cancellation of a domestic debt abroad.

So, let us focus on Z". We will presently diagram its flow in the circuit, but it is best for you to work, as we go along, towards your own diagrams. To the final diagram of chapter three of *Economics for Everyone*, then, there must be added a flow per interval, Z", from the redistribution function to the surplus demand function. It then joins with E" to give a total surplus demand of E" + Z".

What is concretely going on must be figured out slowly. From chapter three you have brought some appreciation of the manner in which E" and (1 − G")O" may surge, etc. But for the moment maintain a focus on Z". Remember that, in our simple case, Z" itself is not a surge: it is a flow per interval which may well be thought of as continuing for colonial decades. We may think, then, of a steady level of plough production per interval, beyond the domestic requirements of maintenance, replacement, expansion. The beyond is, as it were, called out of the local economy by Z". But called in what way?

Focus on the surplus demand, E" + Z". E" is a continuation of a circular flow—let's nor fuss over crossovers here. It comes from outlay and goes to meet outlay, (1 − G')O". For initial simplicity, think of a double steadiness. A plough culture has been established; a plough exporting is also established. Numbers help the inquiring imagination: the economy is producing steadily 110 ploughs, of which 10 are exported. The trick is to notice that the steady state of the economy is peculiar. It is not the steady state of a plough-using island economy, even though the production of ploughs is steady at 110 ploughs per interval. It could help to think the situation out historically, through the beginnings of the venture of export moving the production of ploughs from a steady 100 to a steady 110 after several intervals. But we are thinking here of the situation beyond that surge. The present E" and a corresponding rhythm of outlay are sufficient to keep the higher number of ploughs in production. So now, what of the additional Z" in the next interval? What you must home in on is, indeed, the fact that it is additional, not needed, in a way that should remind you of the discussion of pure surplus income near the end of chapter three of *Economics for Everyone*. So, within the concrete complexity of the effects of the entry of Z" into the circuits, you can recognize its central reality as a surplus income that is the possibility of new fixed investment. Z'' can move to take its place in the redistributive function as that possibility: an unspecified possibility that, of course, need have nothing to do with the production of additional ploughs or new types of ploughs.

Before considering further the circulation of Z'', let us add the same type of favourable balance on the basic level. Instead of the export of ploughs we now consider the export of bananas: it may bring to mind not only the phrase banana republic but also the banana war of 1994 in Europe.[4] Now we have the export of y bananas per interval, with the corresponding movement of Z' into the economy. We now have $E' + Z'$ as basic demand reaching basic supply and you can recognize Z' as being other than a normal component of the production circulation, as a surplus that is the possibility of new unspecified investment. Let us view all this with the help of our fundamental diagram.

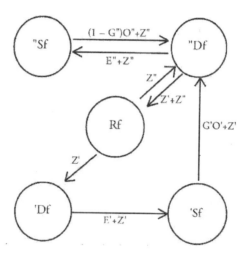

---

[4] The banana war in Europe has colonial roots, for example, the British encouragement of banana farming in the Caribbean colonies. In 1994 the British wished to protect, through tariffs and quotas, those loyal sources from South American producers. The Germans, with no such colonies and an 8 kg per person per year appetite for bananas, were for a free marker. Also on the side of the free market, of course, were the giant producers Chiquita, Dole, and Del Monte, with 60% of the world output. In the 1994 battle, Dame Eugenia Charles, the Prime Minister of Dominica, warned that if islanders couldn't make a living on bananas, they might take up cocaine-production.

It is no harm to remind you, even at this stage, that the diagram is an aid to separating and understanding functions. The circles are not places, nor are they, say, groups of capitalists, workers, bankers, exporters. Recall your pocket of money in chapter three of *Economics for Everyone*. It would be a very worthwhile exercise, as a context for the present chapter, to try to figure out *where*, in relation both to the diagram and to local geography, government is, foreign debt is, the island shoreline is, and where Eurodollars, OPEC monies, World Bank transactions are. How do Z' and Z" *really travel?* What, indeed does *travel* mean in the world of E-Cash?

The diagram represents the functional journeys. I have labeled the parts of the journey for convenience of reference. For simplicity I omit some flows that are concomitant: I will add these when dealing with government operations, but you may well like to work at this yourself. We list, then, the added elements of circulation, tagging on parallel flows:

1a)	Z'	1b)	Z"
2a)	E' + Z"	2b)	E" + Z"
3a)	G'O' + Z'	3b)	(1 − G")O" + Z"
4)	Z' + Z"		

We have, then, (1) Z = Z' + Z" entering the demand function, (2) its expenditure, (3) its identification as surplus income which does not 'immediately demand,' so it is (4) located in the redistributive function. You must satisfy yourself, as best you can, by thinking through concretely or with illustrations, by envisaging export transactions, that the functional journey makes sense. Why, for instance, does not Z move more directly to the redistributive function?

The result of the favorable balance is that, interval by interval, there is a new credit item in the balance of payments of our island. The Z' + Z" per interval was once undifferentiatedly associated with gold importing—you may recall the tradition of mercantilism—but now it is, e.g., a rate of foreign lending, or of the payment of a foreign debt, or the interest on it.

Our simple illustrations leave us far from the concrete complexities of the island's economy, but we can move a step closer to such problems by considering the domestic accumulation of credit in relation to simple surges in the island economy. We have envisaged a steady state of production of ploughs or bananas or both, where a definite fraction is for export. If you think this out in terms of the accumulation of credit, you will be led to suspect that the steadiness is doubtful. The credit is a possibility of expansion, an invitation to some new surging in the economy. The new surging, of course, requires an understanding of surging that mediates a balanced emergence of its benefits: we are back to the problems of chapter three of *Economics for Everyone*. But let us focus on the effect of Z on an island economy that is going through some process of surging. Recall our reflections in chapter one of *Economics for Everyone* on the rhythms of an emergent plough culture, and the financial rhythms necessary for that emergence discussed in chapter three. Now there is added a steady (let's not fuss over this) flow of pure surplus income. It obviously gives a lift to the economy but it does more than that. The details of the extra effects require a return to the analysis of chapter three. But I focus only on major facets of the effects: the energetic reader can probe, e.g., questions of inflationary effects.

So, for example, the increased rate of savings required for a surplus expansion was seen to be a definite problem: the added flow of surplus income eases that problem. But what of the decreased rate of savings that would yield a healthy basic expansion as well as a leveling of the particular surplus surge? It is, I hope, fairly evident that the added flow eases the burden of the decreased rate of savings or rates of losses. But there is a less evident effect. The added flow encourages expansive tendencies that may focus on a prolonged surplus expansion and a dodged basic expansion. The acceleration can focus on an increment in production that sells abroad, so that the need for lowering higher incomes and raising lower incomes is bypassed.

The previous paragraph is a compendious indication of a heuristic attitude which needs enormous filling out. The paradox of that filling out is that it requires its own application to generate precise instances either in history or in planning. The details of the rhythms considered in chapter three of *Economics for Everyone* have to be brought into play in understanding particular situations. Also, of course, more complex local rhythms have to be brought into focus or anticipated, as well as the complexities that are present because of synchronization of cycles of various groups of economies or even larger development lags in economic structures. It is sufficient in the present effort if you begin to glimpse the necessity and the plausibility of the functional analysis for the understanding and guiding of the globe's economy. In its fullness it should become the basis of the factual, contrafactual, and proleptic analysis of the twists and turns of economies in history and of the hopes for global economic development.

However, even if present categories and mindsets are inadequate to the task of homing in adequately on economic history and economic planning, it is still worthwhile to pause over past performances and current trends to at least see the need of the missing perspective.

My reader will have her or his own leads to broader reflection or local illustrations. The reflection or illustrating should have the character of a heightening sense of the need for understanding rather than a yearning for a quick fix. During my work on this chapter I received a letter from a concerned Mexican—it was during the crisis of early 1995 that was *fixed* by the USA bail-out—asking for a solution to Mexico's economic problems from the perspective of the present analysis. My reply was mainly an effort to intimate the need for a massive shift in the understanding of the complex rhythms, history, and geography of production, financing, and trading. One might think here of the parallel in the complexity of motions in the galaxies, or even in the solar system of planets, satellites, projectiles: to understand and control such a complex, one has to leave behind broad Aristotelian ramblings about natural motions and figure out how the moon moves, how the penny drops.

The Mexican crisis is, perhaps, in the reader's past, but an event that coincided with my writing may help you muse profitably about local and global needs. I read in *Time* magazine (wondrously dated March 27th, 1995) of a 'Maestro in the Wings': 'the venerable but much criticized World Bank wins ovations for its versatile new president.' Centre-page is a picture of James Wolfensohn, the new head coach, playing the cello at Carnegie Hall, but of course the versatility includes his 'extraordinary career in financing and public service spanning three continents.' But does he have a fundamental grasp of the normative rhythms of production, finance, trade? Does he appreciate the basis, the bases, or is he set to coach an early form of rounders? Well, that's another story.

The conclusion of the article has a quotation from Robert McNamara, who headed the World Bank from 1968 to 1981: 'The bank needs intellectual leadership with passion, a willingness to defend itself with vigor.' The reference and sentiment lead me back to my memories of McNamara's unenlightened missionary spirit.[5] McNamara was parachuted into the World Bank in 1968, the same year that Bernard Lonergan corresponded with me regarding the need for economic enlightenment. Lonergan had been lead to correspond with me by his sense of the inadequacy of J.B. Metz's political theology which he had been reading. Twenty-five years later, in a rediscovered text of Lonergan's on economics, I found Lonergan's point

---

[5] Deborah Shapley, *Promise and Power: The Life and Times of Robert McNamara* (Boston: Little, Brown and Co., 1993).

made succinctly, equally applicable to McNamara and Metz: "The vast forces of human benevolence can no longer be left to tumble down the Niagara of fine sentiments and noble dreams."[6]

McNamara came from big business and bombers to banking. In 1968, the Bank's annual borrowings were $735 million, the cost to the Pentagon of a few F-111 fighter-bombers, or less than a month's fighting in Vietnam. So McNamara plunged forward, thinking in billions not millions, and it is worth pondering, with the help of a lengthy quotation from Deborah Shapley's biography, over the perspective and direction of his efforts. The quotation also introduces the perspective of Rostow, also worth pondering over in the light of our elementary struggle.

The field of aid had indeed been experiencing 'frustration' and 'failure' when McNamara was parachuted into it in April 1968. The accepted model for how the new countries of Africa, Asia, and Latin America should modernize was based on the presumed lessons of the industrial Revolution and on Western Europe's recovery after World War II. All societies were presumed to go through stages, from subsistence farming to large-scale agriculture, to a bourgeois, small-business phase, to heavy industry. Only in the last stage was enough capital saved and pooled for reinvestment, which could generate more industrial activity and profits: this was the 'takeoff point' at which growth became self-sustaining and the benefits of growth would 'trickle down' to the poor. The text advocating the 'stages of growth' theory was a book of that title, written by Walt Whitman Rostow, who later became Lyndon Johnson's national security adviser and a proponent of bombing. Rostow had been McNamara's nemesis in his last year in office, and now McNamara learned to criticize his theory of economic growth as well.

The World Bank had followed the stages-of-growth philosophy, not because of its intellectual depth, but because it could be used to justify large loans for dams, power plants, industrial activity, telecommunications—in other words, the kind of lending the Bank knew how to do. For much of the 1950s and 1960s, the theory seemed to work: The gross national product of the Third World grew in the 1960s at an average of 5% per year,

---

[6] **FNPE**, chapter 3, section 17, page 36.

which slightly exceeded American and European economic growth.

But theoretical stages of growth and trickle down were not working, as any visitor to India or Africa could see by the late 1960s. Officials who dealt with the repeated tragic famines in India and Pakistan, and the hectic emergency shipments of wheat from Alberta, Canada, or Kansas to prevent mass starvation, knew that GNP growth can hardly be an accurate measure of progress.[7]

A thesis of this small primer leads to the claim that McNamara lacked the basis of criticizing Rostow, of taking the measure of the state of economic play, of performing as a head coach. To the problem of measured coaching we turned in chapter five of *Economics for Everyone*. Here I make the outrageous claim that the basis of serious criticism and construction is lacking in the ruling economic community. Peter Drucker wrote in the eighties, "By now we know, as Schumpeter knew fifty years ago, that every one of the Keynesian answers is the wrong answer."[8] But this *we* does not seem to include the vast majority either of economics professors or economic advisors.[9]

However, we must break off our distractions to get back to our elementary searchings. As I have repeated regularly, the distractions are not really distractions, but aids to the maintenance of our concrete intention, attention: there is nothing abstract about our analysis. So, the transition to our next consideration of our island's balance of trade is helped along by recalling McNamara's dealings with Kenneth Kaunda in the mid-seventies.

Instead of ploughs or bananas we have copper. But now we have the added reality of a plunge in copper prices in 1976. In the crisis the Bank did not pull the plug on Kaunda's Zambia: indeed, the bank went on to fund three unsuccessful agricultural projects. What had McNamara, Kaunda, the economic advisors on both sides, 'in mind' throughout all this? Certainly not a view of two flawed circuits of economic activity, with equally flawed superposed circuits. What was happening in Zambia? What is going forward economically as Zambia moves into the new millennium? What might have

[7] Deborah Shapely, *op. cit.*, note 5, 468.
[8] Peter Drucker, "Schumpeter and Keynes," *Forbes*, May 23, 1983, 125–26.
[9] Paul Krugman, *Peddling Prosperity: Economic Sense and Nonsense in an Age of Diminishing Returns* (New York: Norton, 1994), gives a sobering account of American strategies of the period.

happened? Without the realistic and normative perspective on the grim game that we are reaching for here, these questions cannot receive coherent answers. As we pointed out in chapter five of *Economics for Everyone*, the answers of the future will resemble more the layered pondering and planning of good baseball than the alchemical prognostications of present bankers and professors.

Let us return from these healthy distractions, relevant contextualizations, to our elementary analysis. We have considered the favourable balance of trade. We turn now to the problems of the unfavourable balance of trade. We do not have to cover the same ground again: the circuits remain the same, but now we consider the sum $Z = Z' + Z''$ to be in some way negative. And we can keep the same illustrations, but with a change of focus: our attention, if you like, is on the receiving end, an island receiving the imports. A fuller diagram of the circulations will help our reflections: government operations are still omitted.

We stick with our simple illustrations, distinguishing Z' and Z'' clearly in order to get you used to thinking in terms of these functional distinctions. We focus on ploughs and bananas with the implicit assumption that one is purely surplus circuit, the other basic, although ploughs can be ornaments and banana extracts can serve a surplus function. To muddy the waters round our island, of course, you may puzzle over such an import as the automobile: that import demands a massive functional change of perspective if adequate historical and statistical data for cycle analysis are to emerge. But at present, in this elementary introductory book and effort, we stay as simple as possible.

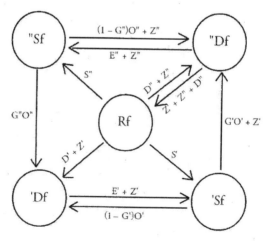

You envisage here, then, that Z' and Z" are both negative, in the sense that some sort of exporting of finance is occurring. Obviously an unfavourable balance of trade can occur with, for example, a large negative Z" and a smaller positive Z'. Indeed, some such situation is entirely plausible, for example, in the case of a less developed nation reaching for expansion. Such cases call for more refined analysis, pointing beyond our introductory struggle. Finally, we hold to our simplification of a steady rate of Z' and Z".

While we could carry through our reflections in terms of a negative Z, it is better—easier and also more systematic—to think of the Zs as positive quantities. So, let us focus first on a steady import of ploughs, Z" per interval, an excess sold on the domestic final market. You have to envisage domestic entrepreneurs directing part of their gross receipts to surplus demand to purchase from the importers the excess imports, ploughs, which are transferred to the surplus final market. In our diagram this is added to the normal circuit flows: 3b: (1 − G")O" + Z" ; 4b: D" − Z", the redistributive connection. The sale of these ploughs corresponds to an addition to normal surplus sales: 2b: E" + Z". Notice that the surplus purchasing of ploughs will actually be more than Z", but such additional costs of domestic production factors—wages, rents, interests, etc.—circulate in the normal fashion. Also, of course, there may be the added complication of incomplete ploughs: they need to be assembled. Again, this domestic complication does not concern us. Z" corresponds strictly to the surplus import and our focus is on its circulation.

There is no serious problem with Z" arriving in the redistribution function. The importers use it to pay foreign sellers in some way through the manipulation of foreign debts or securities. The fundamental problem lies with 1b: D" + Z", the flow of money that is needed to complete the circuit at the other end, that is needed to make the surplus purchase of Z" per interval. You may have to go back to chapter three of *Economics for Everyone* to envisage the problems associated with D", a borrowing per interval for capital equipment. Now we have D" + Z", which includes an additional *borrowing* of Z" per interval, for the maintenance, replacement, or net increment of domestic capital equipment. One can, optimistically, envisage Z" as a 'flow through' from the redistributive function: Z" is being paid per interval for the excess import, received by those borrowing from abroad or benefiting (through interest or principal) from previous foreign investment or—one thinks of earlier times—selling gold abroad. The optimism consists in regarding all these receivers as willing to funnel their funds towards surplus investment, so giving D" + Z". But close attention to what Z" is doing will cool any optimism. It is not, like D", purchasing domestically produced surplus goods, the production of which generates a balancing domestic income. What matches the *borrowing* of Z" is a rate of payment for excess surplus income: it is not *calling out*, lifting, domestic surplus activity. That excess may be towards a capital expansion, or it may be merely replacement capital goods. But in either case we have a weak or sick domestic economy, unable either to accelerate itself or, in the second case, to maintain itself. The weakness may be the weakness of a young economy or it may be that of a settled elder. But in neither case is there a scenario of optimistic investment. Domestic investment is unattractive where domestic capital is on foreign crutches. Depending on the age and state of the economy, foreign debts are increasing or foreign holdings are decreasing. A young resource-filled country may surmount the difficulty. But the old creditor country can settle into a chronic condition needing profoundly unattractive measures. Can you survey the globe for instances? The difficulty here is the absence of the functional classifications, basic and surplus, and the rhythmic ramifications. It is like trying to have a clear view on fire-hazardous chemicals prior to the emergence of the perspectives of Lavoisier and Mendeleev.

However, you have reached something analogous to that perspective from our elementary considerations of the previous chapters. It seems late in the day to swing back to the character of those suggested reflections, and to the question of pedagogy and method, but it strikes me as appropriate to do so here. Bad reading habits die hard, and there may be—you may be—the type of reader who simply reads on steadily, not accepting that my words are pointers towards exercises. So let us pause over the messy pedagogical tackling of this balance of trade problem.

What we are doing has its parallel in those elementary experiments of the beginning of learning chemistry: envisaging and discovering simple reactions, verifying simple reaction equations involving hydrogen and oxygen, simple salts and acids. Just as one does not appreciate such reactions through a single demonstration experiment—one can, of course, memorize reaction equations and pass exams quite mindlessly—so here our simple *Gedanken*-experiment has to be supplemented, sustained, enriched, by a serious imaginative effort and endless scribbles. The comings and goings of ploughs, bananas, finances, have to be puzzled about, all the time latched into a struggle with the flow diagrams.

Though the same diagram covers both flows (does this puzzle you, since we seem to have the *wrong sign* on Z in the unfavorable balance?), it is best to work with different diagrams. The two diagrams of favorable and unfavorable surplus trade 'say' different things to you, with a subtlety that depends on how long you work in the conversation! You, many of you, will still find it difficult to think functionally. So, how do you imagine the activities of the flow represented by the lines corresponding to [A] (1 − G")O" + Z" *going on to* −D" + Z" and so on to R? Not, I hope, in terms of suppliers passing money on to buyers who pass money on to some redistributive area.

Eventually your messing may lead you to view the favorable and unfavorable trading as brought out by ordering the flows differently. In the unfavorable trading, the complex flow, [A], just mentioned, can be seen to get the ploughs in. Then a second flow, [B] completes the circuit: D" + Z" going on to E" + Z". The favorable trade can be envisaged as reversing these two complex flows. [B] first, getting the ploughs out, then [A] completing the circuit. The same circulation, diagram-wise: can you become clear enough on the shift of reading to talk it out concretely, to teach it? A focus on the redistribution area gives the obvious difference: [B] + [A] leads to accumulation in R; [A] + [B] has the opposite result. And so perhaps you can come to grasp my earlier statement that Z was in some way negative in the unfavorable case?

I am pretty sure that, even with an exercise-laden reading, you are not comfortable with all this. Being really comfortable would mean that you are Basically Adequate, B.A., in economics, and would require perhaps three years messing around in the present perspective. To this topic we returned in the Epilogue of *Economics for Everyone*. The point is best noted here in returning to our analogy with chemistry. Trying to get to grips with the simple reactions of hydrogen and oxygen, nitrogen and chlorine, is difficult, a first effort of chemistry far removed from comfortable control of organic chemistry. Our elementary venture into trade reactions is quite distant from comfortable control of organic economics.

Let us turn our attention now to the problems of excess basic importing. We have the same circuit as we had for excess basic export. No need, I hope, to repeat the pedagogical pointers. The central problem that emerges here is the problem of completing the circuit by something equivalent to consumer borrowing. It cannot, under normal circumstances, be sufficiently met by *de-hoarding* and the spending by a rentier class of interest or principal of foreign holdings. Such spending on domestic holdings, of course, is already integral to the domestic circulation.

There is a wide variety of cases of excess basic importing, so let me limit our reflections here to two extreme cases, always within the hypothesis of a fixed Z' per interval. One extreme is that of a necessary excess, the other is what I may call a luxurious excess.

The necessary excess is one easily illustrated by our illustration of banana importing: it envisages the payment of debt, interest or principal, by a banana republic. Our importing island either accepts the bananas, or the case moves into the area of debt forgiveness, repudiation, whatever. You have to think here of a creditor economy gone rentier. There is a past of foreign lending, but now lending does not keep pace with interest and dividends due to former loans, and our banana republic meets its payments with bananas. Now think further of the steady importing in relation to the rhythms of our importing island's economic surges. Suppose the island is in the process of a surplus expansion. Then a failure of the flow 1a is normally all to the good. The actual rate of savings tends to be less than that required for the expansion, and the concomitant excess basic income can be turned to the excess basic import. However, if you put this illustration back into the fuller context of $Z = Z' + Z''$, then the problems of surplus expansion that we noted there will temper a simple optimism about a banana solution.

When the phase of the importing economy is not that of surplus expansion, the failure of 1b, of $D' + Z'$, leans the economy towards depression. The basic monetary flow is not sufficient, at current prices, to meet the flow of goods and services. It is a failure repeated, interval by interval, pushing prices down in the aggregate. Falling prices effect aggregate outlay and income, operations are scaled down, and the fixed Z' becomes increasingly important.

You are, I hope, distracted in your reading of the last paragraph by various facets of the problem, e.g., varieties of price inelasticity, and by possible solutions to it, e.g., government intervention. We are indeed, on the edge of discussing government interventions. But it may be worth your while to go over the paragraph, so to speak, in its primitive simplicity, in a manner closer to the work of chapter three above. Then you think, perhaps, of two small Pacific islands with exchange economies related by a debt problem. You need to think it through to grasp clearly the shifting from equilibrium, the shrinkage of prices. Of course, as you think it through, you will arrive at some puzzling about the unnecessary fixity of the amount of money on each island.

Our discussion, however, has been increasingly in a modern context. And the modern context has its evident solutions to the problem: e.g., force the recipients of interest and dividends on foreign holdings to spend their income on the basic final market. The forcing, of course, is done through taxation of those better off; the spending is done through welfare income. To the problem of fixity of money—which disappeared anyway, in fact but not in theory, with the emergence of primitive banking and credit—there is the modern solution of monetary expansion. Such solutions lead us to some concluding elementary reflections on government operations.

The other extreme case I mentioned, luxurious excess, is a clear instance of the possibility of such an operation on the economy. Think, for example, of the luxurious excess in the concrete terms of our island moving into a fixed frenzy for strange basic imports: Irish spring water, Russian vodka, pet-dog food (what about food for industrial guard dogs?!) from Australia, the perfumes of Arabia and Paris. The luxurious excess has the same effect as the bananas: but here the government can call, Halt. In the case of the bananas, a halt is not that simple. Not that dealing with luxurious excess is simple in these days of free trade negotiations.

You may well find the energy and interest to follow up various other possibilities. The most evident other case is had by turning from bananas to that staple of diet and of economic debate, corn, not now needed to handle a foreign debt, and not a luxury, but a basic need. You might well be led into reflections on nineteenth century Britain, and such a broadening is all to the good, provided you hold our focus. What we seek is a grasp of a missing perspective grounded in the classification that emerged from chapter four above. That is what I wish to lead you to seek, whether you turn to nineteenth century Britain or twentieth century Australia, to Keynes' slim reflections on the trade cycle or Friedman's view on money.

The mention of Friedman leads us comfortably back to our topic, the failure of $D' + Z'$ during a steady unfavorable balance of trade in basic goods. Monetary expansion would seem a way to go. But the way of that expansion is not through an insane steady surging of consumer credit. So, one thinks of expansion in terms of increments in entrepreneurial activity: one thinks of (who might this one be, thinking in terms of two circuits?!) an $S' + Z'$ or an $S'' + Z'$. But does this solve the problem? The products of such increments, and they are predominantly capital increments, reaching the final market, are in competition with the excess import. Still, contraction can be avoided by continued bold monetary policy. The production increments in the surplus market can be bought by surplus borrowers. So, this solution to the problem of providing a $D' + Z'$ involves both a $D'' + Z'$ and an $S'' + Z'$. Interval by interval, there is an increase of debts by $2Z'$: concretely, of course, Z'' has to be taken into account. But let us think through what is going on in that part of the economic flow which we might designate as Z. Clearly, there is an increase of debt per interval of $2Z'$. The Z' to surplus demand can purchase the additional surplus product per interval, and continue circulating to maintain that surplus increment. The Z' to surplus supply function is directed to expand that supply, but its primary achievement is to become the basic income that solves our problem, purchasing the excess basic supply and thus moving back to the redistribution function. The surplus expansion, however, leads to a basic expansion, goods moving to the final basic market, so again the economy is faced with correction. Unless such basic goods can be moved towards export: that, of course, is the fundamental solution to the problem with which we began.

We have been touching on, but dodging, the operation of government right through this problem of the unfavorable balance of trade. Let us now turn our attention to it. Before doing so in our own style, it would be helpful for you to consider a standard elementary presentation of the entire topic of our chapter. It is contained in a diagram from the text by Gordon. The heading of the diagram might well have been the title of the present chapter: 'Introduction of Taxation, Government Spending, and the Foreign Sector to the Circular Flow Diagram.' I include the diagram here on the next page.[10]

---

[10] Robert Gordon, *Macroeconomics*, 6th edition (New York: Harper Collins, 1993), 38.

THE GOVERNMENT SURPLUS OR DEFICIT BALANCES THE REQUIREMENTS OF THE CAPITAL MARKET AND THE GOVERNMENT SECTOR

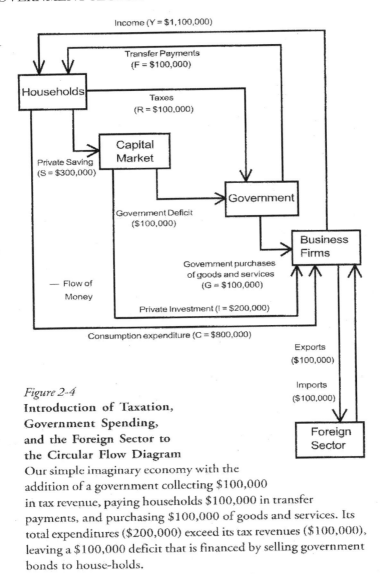

Figure 2-4

Introduction of Taxation, Government Spending, and the Foreign Sector to the Circular Flow Diagram

Our simple imaginary economy with the addition of a government collecting $100,000 in tax revenue, paying households $100,000 in transfer payments, and purchasing $100,000 of goods and services. Its total expenditures ($200,000) exceed its tax revenues ($100,000), leaving a $100,000 deficit that is financed by selling government bonds to house-holds.

Obviously, it would be a very good exercise for you to try to recast the flows so as to bring this diagram into alignment with our own diagrams as they emerge in this chapter, and it seems best to leave the task to you. The effort will help you to move towards the problems of measurement discussed in the chapter five of *Economics for Everyone*. But it will also carry you back to the diagrams and discussions of chapters two and three above. Most evident is the need for the distinctions that emerged from our first efforts in chapter one of *Economics for Everyone*. As we saw there, it is not enough to have just households, businesses, and a national income. If we are to know what is going on in the economy we need to have estimates, historical, and contemporary and future (in layered tentativity), of the aggregates covered by Y' and Y'', basic and surplus incomes. Y, as given in Gordon's diagram, is simply not sufficient to initiate or sustain an explanatory economics. My reader may well be interested in carrying this criticism forward even to invading the sacred fortress of the unmentionable of note 3 of chapter one of *Economics for Everyone*. But at least push towards some level of conviction regarding a fundamental need. Simply sketch our baseball diagram and try to locate the elements of Gordon's diagram in it. For one thing, you will reach a healthier respect both for Lonergan's achievement in isolating the redistributive function and for the complexity of that function in national and international economics. Also you will anticipate the need for the distinctions in government operations that we are about to tackle. The problem of taxation and its effects, for instance, requires a distinction between surplus and basic taxation that goes beyond vague descriptions of personal and business tax. The problem of government spending likewise must be met by the distinctions introduced below between Z' and Z''. And so on: all this requires a massive restructuring of historical and statistical inquiry.[11]

---

[11] The distinctions, of course, are nor unnoticed or un-recommended. See, e.g., Jerzy Osiatynski, ed., *The Collected Works of Michal Kalecki*, vol. 5, *Developing Economies* (Oxford: Clarendon Press, 1993). In the first essay of the volume, "The Problem of Financing Economic Development," Kalecki writes of sectorized taxation (pages 34, 35, 40). His context echoes the reach of our second chapter: "We shall subdivide the economy into two sectors producing investment and consumption goods, respectively. In each sector, we shall include the production of the respective commodities from the lowest stage. Thus, production of raw materials and fuel will be allocated between the two sectors according to the uses that are made of them in the production of final products." *Ibid.*, 23.

But here we must stick with our introductory effort which may seem little more than impressionistic, even though it does cut through to the essential. The diagram immediately following is the object of our attention for the remainder of the chapter.

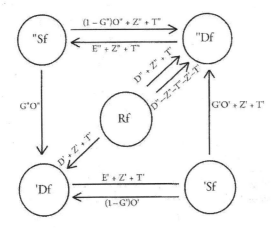

Let us first focus on current government operations without any comment on public debt. Assume steady government spending, interval by interval, of Z' and Z''. This, of course, is the key distinction, making it possible to relate government operations to the operation of the two circuits, basic and surplus. Without the introduction of this distinction, which we keep noting as necessitating new types of data-identification and organization, we simply do not know what is going on, what damage is being done or undone by government operations. The center of the economic problem is that there are two circuits: their continuity in macro- or micro-expansion or in dynamic equilibrium requires that their normative needs be respected, that their respective outlays and expenditures remain dynamically balanced.

So we turn to the very evident zone of government operation, taxation, and distinguish surplus and basic taxation, T'' and T' respectively, again considered as steady per interval. Now let us consider the case of deficit spending, a case massively verified in the past decades in the locale of my writing, Canada and the United States. Z, then, is greater than T, but this is not very enlightening until we view the circuits. Let us take two sufficiently clear situations: in the first case, Z'' is so much greater than T'' that Z' is less than T'; in the second case, Z'' is so much smaller than T'' that Z' is greater than T'.

Both situations are evidently situations in which one circuit is being drained to the doubtful advantage of the other. If Z'' is greater than T'', then the surplus circuit is being urged to expand, inflate, or settle for redistributional deposits. But a squeeze is put on the basic circuit, so that basic prices are pressured down and basic production is discouraged by this and by the high taxation. The economy is coaxed, interval by interval, towards further surplus activity. The situation may remind my reader of the colonial days, except now such a market may be unavailable.

The other situation, with Z'' less than T'', is one which seems more compatible with welfare tendencies. Surplus income, associated with the rich, is taxed more vigorously, while there is an easing of the tax-burden on the less well-to-do. Z' is then the prime outlet for government spending. Z'' is small and overall surplus activity is discouraged. There is nothing surprising in a resulting consumer price-inflation, in a failure of enterprise, in a decline in both employment and stock value.

You will certainly find it useful to think out other situations, and to extend your reflections to real economies, even though the two flows are not acknowledged with any precision in the literature. But such rambling will help you further towards the significance of the elementary distinctions for the understanding of government operations.

Our two illustrations have been of deficit spending, a regular reality after Keynes, climbing to the North American madness we have already noted, with its consequence in a bewildering burden of debt. The Reagan administration doubled government debt from $1 trillion in 1981 to $2 trillion in 1986, and in that period the United States moved from being the globe's major creditor to being the largest debtor. Of course, when we think of debt and debt servicing we are likely to focus on the impossible situation of the lesser developed countries, especially the Latin American debt. You may even be familiar with various suggestions regarding solving the debt problem. It is best to use any such familiarity only to bring forward your appreciation of the need for a change to a scientific perspective: otherwise, as I have witnessed, discussion of the relevance of circulation analysis floats towards the floods of erudite commonsense chat.

So, let us make a very general foray into the question of debt servicing, beginning from the diagram of the processes of government spending and taxation. You have noticed already, no doubt, the parallel between such processes and the favorable and unfavorable balances of trade. For that reason, and to conform with Lonergan's usage in his work, I stuck with the variable Z as the superposed variable. You might well find it convenient, in your exercises, to use more precise terminology, e.g., F (foreign) for international trade, P (polity) for government, especially if you are trying for a total diagram. The process of debt-servicing will normally parallel the unfavorable balance of trade. We are not in need of a new diagram: the only difference in this topic is an added focus on taxation, T' and T", as related to the payment of interest and the provision of amortization. So we have superposed circuits as indicated in the diagram. It is useful to list the components of the total process of government operations:

1) D' + Z' + T'   D" + Z" + T"
2) E' + Z' + T'   E" + Z" + T"
3) (1 – G')O' + Z' + T'   (1 – G")O" + Z" + T"
4) D" – Z' – Z" – T' – T"

First let us attend to the circuit of government spending. The deficit spending by government at all levels—federal, provincial or state, municipal—leads evidently to the first two elements, from the redistributive function to demand. The spending, Z' and Z", shifts a proportion of current production towards public use or even waste—think of rounds of practice ammunition. The income, not spent by individuals targeted by previous outlay, is pure surplus income, which gives elements 3 and 4 on our list. Let us not push further into the possibilities of this surplus income: we may consider it as going to the purchase of government securities. Such purchasing may be seen as curtailing inflation. Of course, one might envisage a perfect taxing system as doing the same thing: but such perfection belongs with the political order of a Plato's kingdom. What we are struggling to see are the consequences of the real mess that economies can move towards, interval by interval. The historical reality of the mess, indeed, is that Z' and Z" are in no way steady, and even the most election-conscious government has to face the vision of a vast rentier class living off the income of government bonds.

So, we have, for example, the problem of enlarging T' and T", at some crisis stage of the history of an economy, where the public debt has mounted, usually at some irregular rare, with tax in the aggregate less than spending. That public debt may be viewed here as unrelieved by any sinking fund, as being a permanently large sum on which interest is paid.

There are certainly inflationary, revolutionary, and capital-levying solutions to the problem, but none of these solutions are associated with confidence in a permanent government. So we must think of the meeting of the issue by massive taxation: T" and T' per interval to meet amortization and to be paid as interest to rentiers. If such taxation is not to contract the circuits—a topic already touched on in some elementary cases—then the fourth element of the superposed circulation must be matched by an equivalent entry into the circuits. What are the possibilities of such a contribution, T' and T", to the first element of the superposed circuit? T' would have to be a mixture of rentier standard of living with a lower income boost through dole, social security, or such: the latter boost itself depending on taxation. T" in element 1 would have to be a rate of investment, balancing the rate of taxation, but still having an accelerating effect in new fixed investment. I will leave you to creatively imagine just how tricky this equivalent entry might be. But granted this first element, the rest follow, carrying forward the inflation of basic income and the flow of surplus income already mentioned.

All this is too hurried, and I have no doubt that you find coming to grips with it, indeed with the entire problem of superposed circuits, quite difficult. It needs a 500-page text, with detailed discussion of instances. As I write, the European community are considering a common currency, but one of the Maastricht criteria for joining is a government debt of less than 60% GDP. Only three countries make the grade, Germany, Luxembourg, and Ireland: the latter only by sleight of hand! Such details, even without our functional distinctions, can help towards entry into the present perspective. One of the benefits of the struggle with them is that it leads you back to chapter three of *Economics for Everyone*, especially to the problem of the nature and possibilities of pure surplus income. The key benefit is to heighten your suspicion that without the distinction of the basic and surplus activities, one is trapped in relatively ineffective description, unable to detect or anticipate local or global economic performance with any accuracy. Of course, the suspicion is there already in the popular mind, crystallized humorously in the search for a one-handed economist, or in the question "How many economists does it take to screw in a light bulb?" The heightening, even after eight chapters, may be little more than an informed glimpse that Lonergan's suggestion is worth following up. His claim, at the end of his own discussion of superposed circuits, is blunt and simple:

> There exist two distinct circuits, each with its own final market. The equilibrium of the economic process is conditioned by the balance of the two circuits: each must be allowed the possibility of continuity, of basic outlay yielding an equal basic income and surplus outlay yielding an equal surplus income, of basic and surplus income yielding equal basic and surplus expenditure, and of these grounding equivalent basic and surplus outlay. But what

cannot be tolerated, much less sustained, is for one circuit to be drained by the other. That is the essence of dynamic disequilibrium.[12]

---

[12] Lonergan, *Macroeconomic Dynamics*, 175, and so also sections 29–31. The discussion there of superposed circuits is complemented by other treatments of the topic, available in **FNPE**. See the index.

9

ORIGINS OF EFFECTIVE SCIENTIFIC ECONOMICS

This little book is about the possible origins of an effective scientific economics emerging from either the Democratic or the Republican Party in the U.S. By now you have caught on to my strategy. Let me recall Chesterton. "A Dublin tradesman printed his name and trade in archaic Erse on his cart. He knew that hardly anybody could read it: he did it to annoy. In his position I think he was quite right."[1] My title was meant to annoy. It might just work. President Trump might see the advantage of getting some of his team to look into this stuff in the serious fashion that I point to at various levels of complexity in this book. He might: but I doubt it, unless he feels challenged or embarrassed. Perhaps his party might push forward in spite of him? Or even the Democrats?

Here, however, my interest is in giving a glimpse of its origins in the odd Canadian, Bernard Lonergan. In a conversation of autumn 1977 about possible success in breaking through, Lonergan remarked to me, "you know, Phil, this is going to take 150 years." Why the strange number? That leaves us 110 years. Still, the Democrats could make a difference. Earlier today I reviewed a Bernie Sanders New York town hall speech of June 23rd 2016, where he talked of an outraged grassroots movement emerging that could beat the establishment and shift wages up. Might I again turn the attention of his disappointed following, to this deeper devotion to outrage? But, realistically, who has the time for this serious effort to fly into a shockingly new scientific perspective? We are back with Kuhn's problem of paradigm shifts in science, except the shift here is from nonsense to science.

There is no point in me rambling even a little through these past centuries of muddling. Enough here to recall Lonergan's muddling along between 1929 and 1944 in quite crazy solitude. He eventually had two decent typescripts, both of which he passed on to Eric Kierans—later a Trudeau cabinet minister—at different times in the 1940s. Kierans admitted to me decades later that he just did not have the time to get into them. Understandable but sad: but what about you?

---

[1] G.K. Chesterton, *George Bernard Shaw*, Bodley Head, London, 1961, 16.

If the *you* reading here is President Trump, I must say that I do not expect you to pause. You have a tough strange road ahead, probably battling even with the Republican Party. Still, as I mentioned in the beginning of the Preface, you might give a nudge or two: ask some serious economist to find out what I am at. But maybe not: then it could be the Democrats who find their way into the great historic Anthropocene science of economics. I think of Hillary Clinton's title and conviction, *It Takes a Village*[2] and muse over some Democrats turning a huge corner by taking seriously the challenge of Bernard Lonergan of 80 years ago:

> The sum and substance of the whole issue is that ideas in the concrete will build you a shanty but not a house and still less a skyscraper. The modern situation demands that questions be settled not in the concrete, not by the petty minds of politics . . . . Physical reality functions perfectly in blind obedience to intelligible law. Humanity must first discover its law and then apply it. To discover the law is a long process and to apply it a painful process: but it has to be done. The alternative is extinction. And practical minds are oriented towards extinction just as much whether they realize the point or not.[3]

My concern in this little book is to turn the practical minds that dominate politics and economics to the genuine practicality that is to invent and give us life in the fullness of the Anthropocene Age. We are back with my musings, in chapter five, on the work of Ian Angus and its inadequacy. And we still have to tackle problems in summary style—again, recalling that fifth chapter with its LOL about the flaws of brief "communication." So, on then, thus warned if not enlightened, on we may go to some sketchy points regarding origins. The little book I have just quoted is the first of two volumes that try for a larger sketch. The second of Michael Shute's volumes is titled *Lonergan's Discovery of the Science of Economics*. It is a shocking but very accurate title.

The story of origin is much larger and more complex than Shute could handle. So I dodge the challenge and give just intertwined pointings about the place of what is called *the Ricardo effect* in the story, which will help to

---

[2] I am recalling Hillary Clinton's book of a decade ago. There is a tenth anniversary edition of *It Takes a Village, and other lessons children teach us*, with a new Introduction, from Simon and Schuster, 2006.
[3] Bernard Lonergan, "Essay in Fundamental Sociology" (1934), in Michael Shute, *Lonergan's Early Economic Research* (Toronto: University of Toronto Press, 2010), 39.

sober and poise our gropings.[4] There is a single entry on that topic in chapter six of the volume just cited, *Lonergan's Early Economic Research*. It is a chapter titled "The Velocity of Money and Turnover Frequency," and a perusal of that chapter would certainly show the directions of really effective groping done by Lonergan, to which I invite you: twelve pages of complex graphs, displays, and equations, which bring a discomforting realism into the climb facing present economists.[5] Shute writes:

> Hayek was interested in the relation between the velocity of money and shifts in the rate of production. This problem was recognized in classical political economy as the Ricardo effect, having been identified by David Ricardo. The Ricardo effect postulates that a rise in wages encourages capital to substitute machinery for labour, whereas a decrease in wages results in the opposite. Hayek reflected on this phenomenon in the light of the trade cycle phenomena, and his reflection led him to consider the time lag involved in bringing a commodity, whether a producer good or a consumer good, to market.[6]

Fred Lawrence, in his lengthy Introduction to Lonergan's *Macroeconomic Dynamics*, also mentions the Ricardo effect, and lists the classical economists who paid attention to facets of this production problem associated with the heavily disputed 'Ricardo effect.' But Lonergan credits Piero Sraffa as having clarified it most thoroughly in his famous essay, *Production of Commodities by Means of Commodities* (1960).[7] Yet even

---

[4] A context on the Ricardo effect is Mark Blaug, *Economic Theory in Retrospect*, 4th edition (Cambridge: Cambridge University Press, 1985), 96–97, 540–46.

[5] A further help here on genuine groping is chapter 14, "Random Pointers," of *For a New Political Economy*, where I gather fragments from this same time of Lonergan's struggle. I would note that the complexities talked of in these fragments certainly involve mathematics, but in a way that weaves in solidly the key variables identified in an initial fashion in chapters two and three above. Present economics is abundant in mathematics, but it is weaved round the muddled generalities that we must seek to escape. It thus remains sophisticatedly muddled "by staying on the same level of generality and by making up for lost ground by going into the more particular fields of statistics, history, and a more refined analysis of psychological motivation and of the integration of decisions to exchange." *For a New Political Economy*, 7.

[6] Michael Shute, *Lonergan's Early Economic Research*, 123.

[7] Piero Sraffa, *Production of Commodities by Means of Commodities: Prelude to a Critique of Economic Theory* (Cambridge: Cambridge University Press, 1960).

Sraffa does not use his sophisticated explanation of the 'Ricardo effect' and the 'roundabout' or 'concertina'-like phenomena associated with it in the way Lonergan does.[8]

This dense little interlude on production-rhythms gives us poise and pause far better than a summary sweep that could detail, yes, years of effort beginning in 1929 and, seemingly, ending after March of 1944.[9] In 1968 Lonergan asked me to find an economist and sent me his 1944 typescript: I am still looking for an economist. In 1978 he returned seriously to the subject, lecturing in the Boston College theology department for five years, basically on modifications of his 1944 typescript. There had been massive changes in his methodological perspective over the decades but in general they remained hidden throughout those lectures. The changes in content are not major but still are too sophisticated for our short nudgings. But one topic is worth airing, since it is central to our relocating of the content in our struggle forward. Our relocating? I think of the unsuccessful presidential candidate's *Hard Choices*, and of her Epilogue remarks. "In the coming years, Americans will have to decide whether we are prepared to learn from and call on the lessons of our history and rise once more to defend our values and interests."[10]

Yes, hard choices: but I write in a different anticipation than Hillary, since I point Americans towards the positive Anthropocene, but in a range of ways to be talked about in Part Three that gives quite new meaning to her 'once more,' indeed cancelling out the 'once more' in favor of novel progress. My challenge to Donald Trump, expressed right at the beginning of the Preface, may, I suspect, be met by arrogant opposition. Still, some way, might there not be some eccentric nudging—a trickle-round effect!— to rise, 'once more' to discover our values and their roots, to cherish our deepest interests, not lightly but with the lesson of people like the Greek Aristotle and the Arab of Damascus and the Italian Thomas and the Canadian Bernard Lonergan, people who point to a future of leisure and contemplation? The road to the new view of profit is one that differs brutally from the habits of research and interpretation and history-lessening that dominate the present Academy.

---

[8] Fred Lawrence, "Editors' Introduction," *CWL* 15, *Macrodynamic Dynamics: An Essay in Circulation Analysis* (Toronto: University of Toronto Press, 1999), lxii.

[9] I included as Frontispiece of *For a New Political Theology* a rare dated—"March 23/ 1944"—page containing a scribble of a set of brilliant equations summing up the dynamic analysis of a single economy. *Ibid.*, xiv.

[10] Hillary Rodham Clinton, *Hard Choices* (New York: Simon & Shuster, 2014), 594.

There is more to be said about Lonergan's work on origins, but best leave the telling to the end of the next chapter, indeed to the rest of the book and the unrest of the Epilogue. Instead of moving on with the grounding of origins by Lonergan, it seems best for me at this stage to turn to a larger perspective on origins that meshes with the life interest of "Hillary Rodham Clinton." The quote-marks point to a little DVD, *Some Girls Are Born to Lead*.[11] It is meant for the open minds of children, but isn't everything? There are many good things in it, including reference to a lecture by Martin Luther King that Hillary attended, but now I wish you to home in freshly on her well-known remark, repeated there, about the lives and drives and rights of women: "the unfinished business of the 21st century." Might I weave in a broader view here? My symbol of the broader view is Joan Robinson, the great scorned economist of the 20th century. Check lists of significant economists; indeed check my list of great thinkers above. These lists fit in with the cute presentation on the Clinton DVD of groups in the 1950s: males all tied up. The male psyche has dominated the axial period and what I call the negative Anthropocene period. Shifting to the positive Anthropocene is an unfinished—or unstarted—business of the 21st century. Might that shift not be boosted by *The Second Sex* in a global freshening of local creativities?

My appeal here is obviously to the candidate who lost the presidency, but who has not lost her way.

---

[11] This is an imprint of Harper Collins, Dreamscape Media, 2016. Written by Michelle Markel; illustrated by Levyan Pham; narrated by Lesa Lockford.

10

Profit II

Let me, let both of us, assume that you actually have now got a decent glimpse of the main point, a point about "the iron laws of economics."[1] The leads came from chapter two, three, and six. The glimpse comes from attending, with illustrations nudging the imagination, to some simple broad examples of innovation: a primitive fruit-gathering community adds a carrying device; a more sophisticated fishing community adds a weir; a later culture leaps to a primitive plough. All the leaps are vaguely recognized[2] as communally advantageous, promising. There is division of labor in realizing the promise and there are rhythms of that realization primitively recognized. So, the sub-group of fishers sidelined into building the weir is to have food for selves and families.

If you like, you can add tokens of promise here. Two elders of the fishing community trying to figure out a decent sharing of fish from new moon to new moon as the weir takes shape. They pause, sitting on a panca or at a banco, and after musing for a while an aboriginal phrase flows from one heart to the other: "we'll have to make a note of this." "We"? The group ferments forward towards this having and this noting. You may even let your

---

[1] The erudite in economic history may chuckle at my trickery here. The initiate may google, but it is not necessary. We are heading in a direction quite foreign to Ricardo, and indeed foreign to Walras, Marshall, Keynes, etc. Joan Robinson was good at sniffing the rotten direction, and Schumpeter was quite precise about missing laws. We touch on their contributions as we move along.

[2] Vague recognition is a characteristic of what I call initial meaning, a fairly nominal grip on a starting point of meaning. Two things are worth noting about it. First, it can be weaved round a density of feeling, and indeed this is an aim of growing meaning. Secondly, its lack of explanatory climbing can be disguised by rich correlating, e.g., with other initial meanings, with other efforts at such enrichment. Such activities ground "academic disciplines" (Lonergan, *Method in Theology*, 3: the concluding words) as opposed to serious comprehensive understanding. The page mentioned just now turns to a next page, (page 4 *ibid.*), that points way beyond present perspectives. One might ask whether economics at present is an academic discipline.

fancy ramble forward to and through the tavern in the town of chapter three: a type of noting that is a broader promise of support from the banco.

"We have to make a note of this." We? You and I and whatever group we may reach: to that I return in chapter fourteen and the Epilogue. Your fancy must ramble openly, even awesomely. I think of Proust listening and tasting freshly.[3] I think of a favorite story of mine about the great conductor Herbert von Karajan. In his seventies he made, as I remember, his second last recording of Beethoven's nine symphonies. When the long editing and splicing was completed, he mentioned to a friend that he was off to Salzburg to conduct the third and fourth. "Will you not be bored?" asked his friend. The answer: "For me they are new symphonies."

In chapter two, three, and six, and in this beginning of chapter ten, we have, you might say, been weaving simple instrument-colors round the five notes that dominate Bruckner's 8th symphony.[4] Now we pause, in the mood of Bruckner, and ask, what might this—the five-pattern—be? What might this be? Is this not a very human question, whether posed about 5 notes or 52 American states? Further, is it not perhaps the only fulsome what-question?

What might this be?[5] Now and here, however, the question points to this 550-word start to chapter ten as the words tumble round, what-gripped in your neuromolecules. This might be a fresh nudging towards reading forward through the chapters that follow chapter three, to find a parallel with Bruckner: my five note-diagram might come to be seen as a hope of

---

[3] See the previous note. The subtle enrichments of writings like Proust's calls out for a fuller context of explanation vibrant with aesthetic meaning.

[4] The five notes are handily written thus, with the subscripted 1 indicting an octave jump down and the hyphen indicating a lengthened doh: doh – me, fah, soh, soh$_1$.

[5] I repeat this question at the end of the paragraph after the diagram, and I sadly know that few will be halted in a significantly serious way by a molecular fermenting of this question that would lift the meaning of profit into a grip on the meaning of its innovative pure fringe as, yes, a loose canon of global prosperity and progress. A few pages further on I invite this same halt in boldfacing nine words: **the potentialities of nature become a standard of living**. Whose standard of living? Might the banker in Joey's village float a surplus promise electronically to a distant village of credit-worthy enterprise? Recall now the quotations from Schumpeter that I gave in note 4, page 14. This is an Oz flight from the Kansas of the "banking industry, which over the past couple of decades has grown vast and insatiable by inventing, for the most part, new ways to market, sell, and invest debt." Ron Suskind, *Confidence Men: Wall Street, Washington, and the Education of a President* (quoted in my Preface, page v above).

dominating the globe's long story as his five notes dominate his 80 minute work. Sing along, then, the basic tune weaved into the simple diagram.[6]

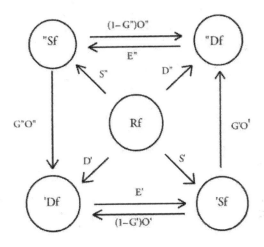

It is best, of course, if you sing with the proper rhythms in mind, in mindingdingding neuromolecules. Then, yes you can reach for a glimpse of the symphony intimated by the global imaging of chapter seven, even if the added imaging of chapter eight is just way too much for you this year, or even this decade. What might this be?

Notice that—perhaps perhaps perhaps—you may have spontaneously bought here into a glorious normativity. The full global buying-in is to be the communal core of the luminously progressive Anthropocene age. It is to bring with it a quite new perspective on the empirical and on empirical method, a quite new empirical and normative perspective on *observing*.

Even though I leap ahead here it seems worth inviting you to observe some late lines of Bernard Lonergan about five other notables of progress: attention, intelligence, reasonableness, adventuresomeness, responsibility. Here you are, yours to **observe**:[7]

---

[6] I leave the weave to you as a very flexible exercise. There are five notes: there are five circles: how best to image the flows—might we say of *dough*?—to and from *me*?

[7] I can only hint at, touch on, satirize, our feeble efforts to **observe**. Chapters thirteen and fourteen will give further pointers. Perhaps the end of note 11 below could give you paws?

Progress proceeds from originating value, from subjects being their true selves by **observing** the transcendental precepts, Be attentive, Be intelligent, Be reasonable, Be responsible. Being attentive includes attention to human affairs. Being intelligent **includes a grasp of hitherto unnoticed or unrealized possibilities**. Being reasonable includes the rejection of what probably would not work but also acknowledgment of what probably would. Being responsible includes basing one's decisions and choices on an unbiased evaluation of short-term and long-term costs and benefits to oneself, to one's group, to other groups.[8]

Notice, observe, and intussuscept glimmeringly, the inclusion, in the dynamic whatting of human intelligence, of adventuresomeness, of a care for what is to come, of the future's promise, whether one is picking up a menu or searching for the Higgs' particle and the benefits of its controlled discovery.[9]

So I return to the suggestion that you may have spontaneously bought here into a glorious normativity. Indeed, you may have bought into it already in chapter three, when you mused over the very sane suggested dynamics of harvesting the ploughs' product. Those of you who have ventured further, even played through Lonergan's 1944 symphony, may not have observed the observation in his first chords about "The Productive Process," where in nine words he slides past the basic Bruckner poise before you rise to the Caucasian. I put the boldfaced nine words in bold face.

---

[8] Lonergan, *Method in Theology*, 53. The boldfacing is mine.

[9] "Menu" is not mentioned casually here. One can get to grips with the quotation just given, from *Method in Theology*, 53, by slowly self-appreciating what happens psychically to oneself, oh-so-swiftly, from the reception of a menu to the satisfied 'I'll have Chicken Kiev' as you hand the menu back. The slowness is symbolized nicely by tackling patiently the existentially-swift climb with Thomas Aquinas through 63 sequential questions on the topic in his *Summa Theologiae* Ia IIae, qq. 6–17. I should note, quite discomfortingly, that this exercise, round the promise of a good meal, points to the massive shift in the meaning of *promise* that is to emerge in this millennium. This relates also of course, to the promise of the Earth, which involves an integral aggregation of scattered promises. A context there is Meghan Allerton, "Functional Collaboration in Ecology," in *Seeding Global Collaboration*, ed. Patrick Brown and James Duffy (Vancouver: Axial Publishing, 2016). Regarding the full dynamic of responsible physics, see Terrance Quinn, *The (Pre-) Dawning of Functional Specialization in Physics* (Singapore: World Scientific Press, 2017).

The activities of the productive process "range from the simple and fixed routines of primitive hunters and fishers to the highly complex and mobile routines of modern Western civilization. Yet in every case there is one effect: **the potentialities of nature become a standard of living**."[10]

The real issue we are dealing with—might I say, Donald and I?—is that America is not great, nor was the "Great Again" of Donald anything but a flawed election gimmick. But perhaps America could start to be great? Might we at least begin, in America, to imagine a shared standard of living that would be quite beyond the present standard of un-life?[11] "A chicken in every villager's pot": certainly. But what of a replacement of Keynes' book of 1936, *A General Theory of Employment*, with a culture of 2036 that would pivot on a General Theory of Unemployment? For, in a sane climb of humanity, employment is to be a shrinking reality. Might we slowly come to promise that it be so?

There is too much more to suggest here, about progress and the full rescuing of every little dollar promise from its axial emergence in dark times, darkened in neurodynamic deadness and sickness in neuroses and pathologies of possession and exchange in a long Ecumangled Age.[12] I would need to weave too much detail regarding the slow subtle climb out of that negative age, that negative Anthropocene Age, to call your hearts in statistical effectiveness towards a patient leisured beginning. That strange hope of us resonating with the cosmic molecules of our hearts and minds will hover over Part Three. So I boldly end here with another writing of 1936, the seed of a later culture of unemployment.

> The function of progress is to increase leisure, that men may have more time to learn, to conquer material evil in privation and sickness, that men may have less occasion to fear the merely factual, and that they may have more confidence in the rule of

---

[10] *For a New Political Economy*, 232.

[11] I have regularly repeated Lonergan's words at the end of a lecture on the importance of art "when philosophers for at least two centuries, through doctrines on politics, economics, education, and through ever further doctrines, have been trying to remake man, and have done not a little to make life unlivable" (*Topics in Education*, University of Toronto Press, 1993, 232). The difficulty we have is in intussuscepting this inhuman state of modern life. Our crippled imagination settles for a shocking low level of normality. Does it help to muse over the Borg Collective of *Star Trek*? Or Seven of Nine's troubles in the sequel, *Voyager*?

[12] I am recalling the fourth volume of Eric Voegelin's series *Order and History: The Ecumenic Age* (Baton Rouge LA: Louisiana State University Press, 1974).

intellect to struggle against the inherited capital of injustice which creates such objective situations that men cannot be truly just unless first the objective situation is changed, and finally—I am not certain I speak wildly—out of the very progress itself to produce a mildness of manners and temperament which will support and imitate and extend .... the virtue of progress, the virtue of social justice, by which man directs his actions so that it will be easier for his neighbor and his posterity to know and to do what is right and just.[13]

---

[13] Lonergan, "An Essay in Fundamental Sociology" (1934), in Michael Shute, *Lonergan's Early Economic Research* (Toronto: University of Toronto Press, 2010), 42–43.

Part Three

Remote Goals

11

AMERICA GREAT, HUMANITY GREAT

Could it be true that an American greatness could lead to the greatness of humanity, whatever that is? Certainly it could: but it depends on the attitude of Americans. Might they possibly rise to a common tuning into "a readaptation of the whole existing structure"?[1] Election rhetoric was the usual mix of better opportunities for all to live what we usually call a successful life, looking back to ancestral values, looking forwards to children that climb to some similar success. All comfortably vague, unless one takes account of particular cultural or religious aims and destinies with the presently impossible serious efficiency that is the topic of this Third Part of the book. We will begin to pause over such particularities in chapters fifteen and sixteen, but now it seems appropriate for me to pose a key strange and discomforting question: "Do you view humanity as possibly maturing—in some serious way—or just messing along between good and evil, whatever you think they are?"[2] This is not a question that weaves into any present political vision of the future. We, all of us, just mess along. In this part of our venture we muse on a road that would lead out of the messing. In the following Part Four we return to the messing leading to and beyond 2020 visioning. Might we seed something that might break beyond the mess to a quite new type of greatness? Was Senator Bernie Sanders on to something? But let's leave that too-close question for Part Four. Except note, as a beginning here: that his seeding failed. Or did it?

So let us fly high and ask, "What sort of seeding—and perhaps seething—would succeed, in some decent statistical sense, indeed, perhaps only in a very long-run sense?" Such long-run thinking is already implied in my principle of the previous paragraph when answered positively: let us call

---

[1] Lonergan, *For a New Political Theology*, 6.

[2] I have raised the question in many contexts, but the relevant one here is that referred to in the next note, which adds a note of concrete fantasy to present shrunken formulations of humanity's right's road. Below in the text I come to suggest calling it *Amendment A*.

it *Amendment* **A**, and might it not be added to all constitutions?[3] Amendment **A** pushes us to think of the total future, something that may seem quite odd. Less odd is the push to think of the past in a somewhat similar way. Democratic Convention talk in Philadelphia weaved its way occasionally round the glory of the creation there, 240 years ago, of America, by its founding fathers. But should we not ask about these fathers and their community's place and poise in the full story of humanity if we are thinking of American greatness as someway paradigmatic? They pushed forward to define institutions of nationhood within the context of a fresh view of liberty. What is that pushing.

Did that four-word sentence—lacking an expected question mark—halt you in your trek? I have brought you back creatively to two first sentences of Joan Robinson's little book, *Freedom and Necessity*, cited earlier. "This book is intended to provoke inquiry rather than to give information."[4] "Consider the profiles of a dolphin and a herring."[5] These sentences, leaning on my previous four-word sentence, bring us nicely to the first sentence of my most recent book dealing with the full problem, the full human task.

> The emergence of humanity is the evolutionary achievement of sowing what among the cosmic molecules. The sown what infests the clustered molecular patterns behind and above your eyes, between your ears, lifting areas—named by humans like Brocca and Wernicke—towards patterned noise-making that in English is marked by 'so what?'"[6]

The title of the first chapter of *Allure* is "Sow What." The history of Europe and its colonies sowed particular whats in the molecules of those founding fathers. They became an institution searching for the structure of institutions, roles, and tasks that would ground liberty in a complex good of order. Let me offer now an array of words that helps us to move forward here. And note that my array invites you to a creative paralleling with some

---

[3] Fancy that being a topic in governments searching for its grounds? Amendment **A** hovering over the right to bear hearts? This may strike you as wildly unreal, especially if you tune into present patterns of U.S. government Middle-East dishonesty (see notes 5 and 20 of chapter fourteen below, following up on Chomsky's stand on Israel). See also note 14 below.

[4] *Freedom and Necessity*, 5. This is the first sentence of the Preface.

[5] *Ibid.*, 9. The first sentence of chapter 1, "The Origin of Society."

[6] Philip McShane, *The Allure of the Compelling Genius of History* (Vancouver, BC: Axial Publishing, 2015), 3. The title of that first chapter is "Sow What."

equivalent array of words generated out of the founding fathers deliberations. Can you enter into a fantasy about structuring all such deliberations in history as part of our global way forward?

capacity	cooperation	particular good
developed skills	institution	good of order
liberty	personal relations	terminal value

Simple illustrations give sense to the display. A family has the capacity, which we can think of also as a need, to produce the particular good that is an adventurous day's outing.[7] Might it become a regular element in their lives? Then it is an institution within the good of order that is their lives together, weaved round skills developed in and towards the steadiness of that institution in context. The two words, "in context," lift our thinking into the third line.[8] The context is their story within the story of humanity. It is an incomplete story, for the small group, for the total tribe: like an unfinished symphony. The capacity, the what wrapped in molecular momenta like sexuality, is then an incomplete liberty reaching for a distant terminal fullness of personal relating. Think helpfully of a concrete symphony, or some beginning of a favorite song. There are the first five words of the American national anthem; there are the central five notes of Bruckner's great 8th symphony.[9] Where are these five going? The grouped capacities of liberty can only reach out of the incompleteness to heuristic sketchings of the goal. Like a little sunflower stem looking for the future brown and yellow face: and perhaps mistaking for it *The Yellow Rose of Texas*. Did the founding fathers get it right? Or was John Wayne's mood too close?

These last two sentences, ending with question marks, are meant only to raise your what, even fleetingly. No one would be so foolishly patriotic as to claim that the founders got it right for all time: certainly not for the ladies,

---

[7] Chapter one of my *Futurology Express* (Vancouver, BC: Axial Publishing, 2013), "The Turn-Around," begins with an invitation to muse over this situation, a musing that could lead you to see and be seized by the fact that "this is the way to the musey room" (James Joyce, *Finnegans Wake*, 6), indeed the way towards hearing "the music of the spheres." Shakespeare, *Pericles*, V. i. 228.

[8] Note here the problem that haunts print. Did the two words "in context" even register fleetingly in your questing? The shift, the leap, to a third-line that breaks with the present flawed good of order is the global task pointed to in this little book. We shall return to the spread of words again, in chapters fourteen and sixteen.

[9] See note 4 above, page 78.

certainly not for the darker skinned. But my existential push now is, how far might your **what** reach regarding getting it right?

Might your **what** pick up on a Toynbee or a Voegelin or a Sorokin in sniffing round the problem of getting it right? Karl Jaspers thought there was a basic right move in humanity during a period that he called *axial*: 800 B.C. to 200 B.C.[10] Toynbee thought it odd that such an axial period would leave out both Jesus and Muhammad. Voegelin saw little advance in Hegel's view of progress from the Sumerian king-listings of 2000 B.C.[11] Sorokin saw that, far from what-focusing in the Greek mode, we had settled into a sensate culture. Perhaps the axial period of humanity is a much longer teen-time of humanity, with the founding fathers tinkering gallantly with a Frenchified nominalism of Plato and Jesus?

These are vague questionings bringing us a context for pausing over the centuries since the founding fathers. Are we to struggle along in an ungrounded optimism, or might there bubble up, in our exploration, **The Complaint** of my early misquotation from Marx?[12] Might our share of **The Complaint** bring us to Lonergan's view of the exploration?

> That exploration is extremely important in our age, when philosophers for a least two centuries, through doctrines on politics, economics, education, and through ever further doctrines, have been trying to remake man, and have done not a little to make human life unlivable.[13]

---

[10] It adds to our context to hear the point from Lonergan: "I have been repeating to you, in my own manner, something like the contention put forward by the German existentialist thinker, Karl Jaspers, in his work, *The Origin and Goal of History*. According the Jaspers, there is an axis on which the whole of human history turns; that axis lies between the years 800 and 200 B.C.; during that period in Greece, in Israel, in Persia, in India, in China, man became of age; he set aside the dreams and fancies of childhood; he began to face the world as perhaps it is." "Dimensions of Meaning," *Collection*, ed. Frederick Crowe and Robert Doran, vol. 4, *Collected Works of Bernard Lonergan* (Toronto: University of Toronto Press, 1988), 237–238.

[11] Eric Voegelin, *The Ecumenic Age*, vol. 4 of *Order and History* (Baton Rouge, LA: Louisiana State University Press, 1974), 68; see also *ibid.*, 7, 27-28, 173. For a fuller discussion see my "Middle Kingdom: Middle Man (T'ien hsia: I jen)," chapter one of *Searching for Cultural Foundations*, edited by Philip McShane (Washington, DC: University Press of America, 1980), 1–43.

[12] See the Preface above at page iv.

[13] Bernard Lonergan, *Topics in Education*, CWL 10, 232.

But what would the adequate effective exploration be? Certainly it would need to reach beyond America as a topic and Americans as a collaborative group. Might we think of it as the core of a science of humanity, leaping, in our imagination and indeed our hope, quite outrageously beyond Plato's dreams and the dreams of the founding fathers?

It seems wise for me to halt abruptly this chapter's dreaming here and now. I ask you to re-read the first eight words of the previous paragraph: "these are vague questionings bringing us a context." Bringing us a context? Bringing a vague hint of a distant "impossible dream" [14] into our "conventional humbug," [15] where, yes, *conventional* is nicely ambiguous, nudging you to recall the party conventions of the summer of 2016. What is the here-and-now context for bringing us to the dream context? "It is in this context that the profound significance of satire and humor comes to light. For satire breaks in upon the busy day. It puts printers to work, competes on the glossy pages of advertisement, challenges even the enclaves of bright chatter."[16] Might we compete with the bright chatter of Wolf Blitzer as it weaves its conventional way round glossy advertisements?

So I pass the baton of the impossible dream of this chapter on to the next. But please please note with some humor my madness, playing, with wit, Plato's grim game of trying to educate Dionysius, who began his rule of Syracuse in 367 B.C. His philosophic uncle, Dion, brought in Plato as teacher: the idea was to bring forth an archetypal philosopher-king. It didn't work. Recall Plato's view:

> Unless philosophers become kings in the cities or those whom we now call kings and rulers philosophize truly and adequately and there is a conjunction of political power and philosophy . . . there

---

[14] Strangely, my mind leaped here to a performance I attended in New York of David Wasserman's 1964 *The Man of La Mancha*, a show having a new run at present. Is there not a quixotic reach in each of us, an evensong of New York putting an edge to the daze of the Big Apple, of the U.S.? Might you and I not fancy, with Wordsworth, every common sight finding freshness in our common Global Apple spinning round the sun? Even in a country whose government stands against decent dreams? See note 3 above on page 86. Might our fancy not ferment into global care?

[15] Lonergan, *Insight*, 649. These pages nudge us towards humor and satire.

[16] *Ibid.*, 648–49.

can be no cessation of evils . . . for cities nor, I think, for the human race.[17]

The idea is massively transformed by Lonergan's view of situations to which we now turn. Are we into impossible dreaming when we think of people running for American government breathing the air of Amendment **A**, the right to bear hearts? Might the idea work, a new right idea, a new idea of right? Well, let's brood in these next three chapters over the long-term shift in culture that is envisaged.

But you should note, pausing, paws in politics, that here, or in these next chapters rather, you begin to see the strategy of my title. The two candidates in the presidential election felt they had the right to expose each other's inadequacy. The feeling was shared by media and by general gossip. Nothing of this exposing seems to have had, indeed to ever have, effect. That is the problem that we face, and we face it with the perspective offered by Plato. Yes, there is the perspective offered by Lonergan, a perspective that claims the problem should be faced, and could be faced effectively. My title, and this wandering essay, emerges in the context of his solution, talking of his solution to king or queen, king-makers or queen-makers, to you. In terms to be described in the next chapter, I am operating in a situation room that has yet to come to be: the eighth—in reality it is to be a population of local rooms—in a cyclic sequence that is to roll humanity forward towards "a conjunction of political power and philosophy."[18]

---

[17] Plato's *Republic*, Book V, 473c11–d6.

[18] See the full text of Plato referred to in the previous note.

12

THE SITUATION ROOM: THE STUPID VIEW OF WOLF BLITZER

You surely recall, in reading this title, the title of my book, and the point made at the beginning of the Preface about attention-getting. The focus there was Donald Trump, yet the reach was into the full context of his Oval Office. Now we are in another room, in the complex collaboration of CNN symbolized by Wolf Blitzer's *The Situation Room*. Is the stupidity there at a much higher—or should I say lower?—level than in the surrounding aggregates of situations that is the American culture? Certainly, the hundred days between the party conventions and the election brought us, and *The Situation Room*, low in a range of ways.

Yet, strangely, it can bring us high, to heights of future human achievement and aspiration. So, while you and I could weave humorously round the presuppositions and the performances of *The Situation Room*, let me rather turn our musings towards glimpsing those heights. I wish you, of course, to resonate self-luminously in a molecular twinkling carry-over of humor and fantasy from the end of the previous chapter as I sketch positions of a strange culture in a very distant positive turn of this Anthropocene Age.

> Humor keeps the positions in contact with human limitations and human infirmity. It listens with sincere respect to the Stoic description of the Wise Man, and then requests an introduction. It has an honest admiration for the blueprint of Utopia, but it also has a vivid imagination that puts a familiar Tom and Dick and Harry in the unfamiliar roles.[1]

I am involving us in the blueprinting of Utopia. A twinkle in the molecular tail of your eye can synesthetically lift your listening.

Especially is this true when I admit to you that there was a twinkle in my own eye when I leaped outrageously from memories of *The Situation Room* to what for me has become a powerful imaging of the future dynamics of

---

[1] Lonergan, *Insight*, 649.

humanity's journeying. My struggle was in the context of the incomplete effort of Bernard Lonergan to trace the structure of that future dynamics. Indeed, it was in the context of a single page very late in that sketching, a page in which he repeats the word *situation* seven times.[2] He had climbed, in that book, through a sketching of seven separable stages of sequential collaboration that would lead to a final eighth stage of getting the drive towards a realizable utopia into town and gown. "Without the first seven stages, of course, there is no fruit to be borne. But without the last the first seven are in vain, for they fail to mature."[3] This last stage he called, lacking a better word, "Communications," [4] but perhaps you would be more comfortable here with the name, "Executive Reflection." You might even stick with our musing on *The Situation Room*, and then find your way easily to name the two prior stages in moving the doings of *The Situation Room* effectively into particular presentations and performances. In fact, if you muse on the concrete faulty reality of CNN, you probably find that there are three different rooms involved for, yes, Policy, Planning, and Executive Reflection.

Nor do you have much trouble in finding me in quite another room, which I call here, but not just for a laugh, "the musey room."[5] Is there a musey room in CNN? In the White House? Recall my earlier mention of Plato nudging Dionysius and ending up in "room arrest."[6] Move round in your own culture, be it from ancient China or from a modern shrunken business of making, entertaining, educating: might you detect some arrestings?

What is my musing, shared with you here, about? It is about a grounding of all room-activities in an answering of the question, "What is humanity?" Or should I not say, in facing the fact that **what** is humanity. "Krishna, what defines a man?" asks Arjuna, and Krishna might well have

---

[2] The page in question is ten pages from the end of Lonergan's effort to give theologians a popular impression of Utopia: *Method in Theology*, 358. Note that with seven repetitions there are eight occurrences of the word *situation*.

[3] Lonergan, *Method in Theology*, 355. I would note that this stand is in coherent continuity with his including implementation in his definition of metaphysics two decades earlier: "explicit metaphysics is the conception, affirmation, and implementation of the integral heuristic structure of proportionate being." *Insight*, 416. That conclusion pushed him to a search for an effective dynamics, named in the final section of chapter seven as an unknown X, Cosmopolis.

[4] The title of the final chapter of *Method in Theology*.

[5] "This is the way to the musey room," James Joyce, *Finnegans Wake*, 8.

[6] Recall the conclusion to the previous chapter.

just said, "Yes!"[7] You, reading along, are a lonely molecular **what**, battered by conventions—yes, Republican or Democratic too—and I, like Ezra Pound, arrested in his day,[8] am writing a *Commission*.

> Go, my songs, to the lonely and the unsatisfied,
> Go also to the nerve-racked, go to the enslaved-by-convention,
> Bear to them my contempt for their oppressors.
> Go to those who have delicate lusts,
> Go to those whose delicate desires are thwarted,
> Go like a blight upon the dullness of the world.
> Go in a friendly manner,
> Go with an open speech,
> Be against all forms of oppression.[9]

The poem should give us pause. In what way nerve-racked? What delicate lusts and desires are thwarted? What dullness? And what friendliness? What, what, are the forms of oppression? How are the musey songs to go, and indeed from whence are they to come? Did you maintain the resonance talked of in the second paragraph above, or even find the eye-vibes and aye-vibes poem-pawings you? Might you be becoming an enfleshing of a Gaia goya against all forms, informs and outfits, of oppression: starting with the self-oppression that would have you not-pause, not knot-paws in poising. Now. Then. "THEN."[10] Maybe even "lay ever, waiting the golden rain."[11]

We may sadly think of Pound as having a brilliant glimmer of a solution, but notice first his own long search for whence it comes: his climb through

---

[7] *Bhagavad Gita*, translated by Barbara Stoler Miller (New York: Bantham Books, 1986), 37.

[8] Indeed, put in a six-foot-by-six-foot outdoor steel cage, May 1945.

[9] An extract from *Commission*, a poem I have quoted in full in *Music That Is Soundless: A Fine Tuning for the Lonely Bud A*, 3rd enlarged ed. (Halifax: Axial Publishing, 2005), 29.

[10] The title of my *Cantower* 5 is "Metaphysics THEN," the beginning of my own pointing of Cantowers, available at: http://www.philipmcshane.org/cantowers. The poem which leads into that *Cantower* is one of Samuel Beckett's last: "go where never before / no sooner there than there always / no matter where never before / no sooner there than there always."

[11] Ezra Pound, *Canto IV*, *The Cantos of Ezra Pound*, one volume edition (New York: A New Directions Book, 1970), 16. I skip past Pound's link with Major Douglas's view, and his criticism of Joyce's disinterest in economic theory.

117 *Cantos*.[12] Look back now to the previous chapter, at the text above notes 6–10,[13] and sniff the fuller reach of such a climb. Is such a reach not now made obvious to us in a simpler way when we think of the reach of modern physics, maturing towards reaching data from the first cosmic second on, a reach that battles collaboratively[14] for an understanding that is correct: and thus, correct, a guiding light for further reachings of searching and inventions? Pause here, in the golden rain, to get a lift of genius that twines with Pound's pounding heart. For, the guiding light in physics: is it not policy, the culture of straining forward?

So, we find, upside down, our last three rooms of Policy, Planning and Executive Poise, in the older rooms of scientific reaching that speak over the centuries of Verifying Theory in Instances: a parallel that needs serious thinking out and in. But see how we need even to rescue those three, so dully and duly named, from "all forms of oppression."[15] The instances of fire burning and plants growing baffle us, so that we may search and research for centuries, what-focused in data, to reach an interpretation or understanding that is correct, verified, that fits the stories of planets and plants.

See, now; seize now: we have found the seeds of seven rooms that would care for proper firing, boiling, growing, lust, a propriety that would stand against tepid, wilting, lack-lustered lackeys of convention. Might we conveniently name the result so far, this layering of seven rooms hovering over every situation, *the magnificent seven*? : Research, Interpretation, History, Musing, Policy, Planning, Executive Poising. Thus we find a context of what's ongoing. But now, a stance emerges, my stance in my musey room, a musey room not listed in the seven.

Is *The Situation Room* a matter of the glossy performances of lack-lustering lackeys of convention? Did the party conventions of the summer

---

[12] It was his climb through the *Cantos* that inspirited me to tackle a parallel series of 117 *Cantowers* in 2002, one per month. It grew to 158 essays in the following decade: see *Field Nocturne Cantower* 43, "The Full *Cantower* Series," available at: http://www.philipmcshane.org/field-nocturnes-cantower. We return in the Epilogue to the need for such contemplative climbing tactics. Think, for example, of Shostakovich's 15-quartet project spread over more than three decades.

[13] Above, pages 86–88.

[14] The massive global venture towards understanding and detecting the Higgs particle is well documented and popularly appreciated. The difficulty is to envisage with effective concrete fantasy understanding and detecting the human complex of particles. We shall pause further over this in the Epilogue.

[15] The conclusion of the poem at note 9 above.

94

of 2016 thus also lack seed and heed? Might things be different in 2020 vision?

I seek to lead you, by that paragraph of questions, to suspect that there is room for another situation room in our line-up of caring rooms: a split in the musey room. For those questions of the previous paragraph divide us into nay and yea. Might we place the occupation of that room between story-telling and musing and name it *dialectic*: not some Marxist thing, or some business of philosophies or theologies, but a simple battling with different stories of progress acted out by communities? "Our interest is not in dialectic as affecting theological opinions but in dialectic as affecting community, action, situation."[16] But that interest places this named dialectic as a part of a vortex of caring, a vortex of situation rooms, the Grate Eight, that is to sift and grate cyclically the global community's affects and actions: Research, Interpretation, History, Dialectic, Musing, Policy, Planning, Executive Poising. There is always in history a scattering of grating and groaning and filing that we may name *Complaining*. But now we may see our way into lifting such planning and complaining into a creative and effective cycle. So we arrive at admiration of, and creative magnetic insight into, Ezra Pound's sniffing out Vorticism a century ago: "if you clap a strong magnet beneath a plateful of iron filings, the energies of the magnet will proceed to organise form. . . . the design in the magnetised iron filings expresses a confluence of energy."[17]

---

[16] Lonergan, *Method in Theology*, 358.
[17] Ezra Pound, "Affirmations, Vorticism," *The New Age: A Weekly Review of Politics, Literature, and Art*, n.s., vol. XVI, no. 11 (January 14, 1915), 277.

13

FACULTIES OF CULTURE

The need to create sound syntheses and systematizations of knowledge, to be taught in the 'Faculty of Culture,' will call out a kind of scientific genius which hitherto has existed only as an aberration: the genius for integration. Of necessity this means specialization, as all creative effort inevitably does; but this time, the man will be specializing in the construction of the whole.[1]

Ortega y Gasset had in mind, when he wrote those words, a quite ambitious shift of academic culture, though a shift that brings to mind Plato's searchings, and also perhaps shadows in other distant cultures like Mo Ti. I am thinking here of, nudging you here to, an imagining of, a much broader and deeper global shift. I find, in my Webster's dictionary, nine genera of meanings for the word *faculty*, all relevant here: the faculty of hearing, the faculty to make friends, mental faculties etc., as well as an academic unit. All such meanings are relevant to the Anthropocene shift I have in mind, but perhaps the shock of the shift can be, literally, sensed, pointed to in a layered way by first thinking of mental faculties rather than, say, academic faculties. Then I am asking you to imagine imagination, moving frighteningly from the word *imagination* beyond the named image to an imaging of the billion-particle complex superficially indicated by some brain diagrams. As you image vaguely that neuromolecular complex, I would ask you to stretch, yes, stretch that same neuromolecular mental faculty complex in you, to recall complexes considered descriptively in an original fashion by Freud and Jung.

I am thinking particularly of chemical patterns associated with the superego, chemical patterns that are eventually to be identified with what I call *the axial superego*.[2] It is a dominant reality, particularly in the first world,

---

[1] José Ortega y Gasset, *Mission of the University*, translated with an Introduction by Howard Lee Nostrand (Princeton: Princeton University Press, 1944), 72.
[2] I have written of the axial superego in various places. See, e.g., *Humus* 2: "*Vis Cogitativa*: Contemporary Defective Patterns of Anticipation," available at: http://www.philipmcshane.org/humus. Don't be put off by the archaic reference.

but trickling and pushing into the other worlds so as to give a global resistance to initiating the forming of the globally-effective faculty of culture that is to fulfill Ortega y Gasset's dream.

We are looking, then, towards, round, at, the physico-chemical conditions of emergence of "a kind of scientific genius which hitherto has existed only as an aberration: the genius for integration." Such genius, yes, can emerge as an evolutionary sport, but the lift of this present beginning of the Anthropocene age from obscene to scenically effective requires the spread of that genius through the evolutionary eduction named *education*.[3] The spread eventually is to be a global reality, fostering the neuro-orientation even of the pre-natal towards free and far-reaching freedom.

> Normally, we think of freedom as freedom of the will, as something that happens within consciousness. But the freedom of the will is a control over the orientation of the flow of consciousness, and that flow is not determined either by the environment, external objects, or by the neurobiological demands of the subject. It has its own free component. Art is a fundamental element in the freedom of consciousness itself. Thinking about art helps us think, too, about exploring the full freedom of our ways of feeling and perceiving.[4]

The quotation ends a lecture on art, and leads us back to the problem of seeding the various global faculties of culture. "Arts as the Core of Future Science" is a topic I have grappled with elsewhere.[5] And I have used such situation rooms as the arenas of the X-Factor and "America's Got Talent"

Indeed, the faulty power—or tower!—has to be conceived in a full contemporary molecular heuristic. It lurks there, a ground of therapeutic resistance and the block discussed by the Kuhn school. Its neural tentacles make general bias the only sane what-life, so that we are cozy with conventions of initial meanings and acquired meannesses. It is the head-shrunk pilot of the present character-politics at the pole opposite to that of the *Magna Moralia* (see note 11 of the Epilogue, p. 139).

[3] The COPON exercises of the next chapter give beginners pointers towards the massive needed lift in education. That future education is to be dominated luminously and self-luminously by the COPON Principle: "When teaching children geometry, one is teaching children children." And, of course, the teacher is teaching the teacher, climbing further into the cloud nine of the poise against the oppression talked of in the previous chapter, starting with Ezra Pound's poem on page 93.

[4] Lonergan, *Topics in Education, CWL* 10, 232.

[5] See *Bridgepoise* 3 and 10, available at: http://www.philipmcshane.org/bridgepoise.

to hint at the conventional brutalization of our nerve-racked dully-and-duly busy underpaid lives. These arenas are radiant with longing.

Surely at this stage of even a light reading of this little book there is a glimmer of a quite new meaning to the word *underpaid*: an established oppressive failure of nature's promise, nature's and *paideia's*. Paid? Paid in subtle haughtiness dollar-sheets that sheet-anchor us in a permanent emergency of un-life. Nature's promise and *paideia* are towards evolutionary joy: memories of such promise are in our molecules, "our arms and legs filled with sleeping memories,"[6] drugged, drained, over-consumptive hopes.

Is there a conspiracy, beyond conventions of habit and laziness and conventions of settling down, not up, that holds us thus in chains? Might we be brought up, nerves unshackled in what-laced brain-molecules by simple shifts in paideiad, pedagogia, Go Gaia? There is no need for conspiracy when we live in Anthropocene blindness: "Everyman completely blind / To the truth about his mind."[7] Still, there is the conspiracy of structured academic staleness, and there are more open conspiracies in educational orientations such as "the Better Battle Plan"[8] of the Koch tradition. "The Kochs were also directing millions of dollars into online education, and into the teaching of high school students, through a non-profit that Charles devised called *The Young Entrepreneurs Academy*."[9] Kevin Gentry focuses the point: "The students that graduate out of these higher-education programs populate the state-based think tanks and the national think tanks."[10] Can dark philanthropy thus rule the waves and ways of generations of whats? Is the best we can do just an opposing of such darkness with some white philanthropy? Should we try taxing dark philanthropy's source out of its existence?[11] And if this is the road ahead, then are we not into Marxist clash

---

[6] Marcel Proust, *Remembrance of Times Past* (New York: Random House, 1932), vol. 2, 1042.

[7] Patrick Kavanagh, "The Paddiad," *Collected Poems* (London: Martin Brian and O'Keefe Ltd, 1964), 90.

[8] "Selling the New Koch: A Better Battle Plan" is the title of chapter 14 of Jane Mayer's *Dark Money*, pages 354–80.

[9] *Ibid.*, 365.

[10] *Ibid.*, 365–66.

[11] I am recalling Piketty's suggestion. It is not a simple bureaucratic matter but a huge central topic of cultural change and re-education regarding sane incomes. Conventions of rewarding of our times are pathological, and there are simply no norms regarding income flows within present economics.

of classes as a permanent absence of a communal, unequally balanced,[12] global care of livable levels of satisfaction?

The challenge to which this book points is one of stirring our neurodynamics to reach for a new synthesis of care, a quite new *nomos*[13] of global humanity, a fresh generalization of the processes and promises of exchange. Part of my pointing is that the challenge has been met but only as an unapplied and solidly ignored generalization.[14] It involves a leap beyond conventions of slim thinking, thinking indeed caught in initial meanings,[15] to quite new living-styles of human interest, satisfaction, leisure, benevolence.

The vast forces of human benevolence can no longer be left to tumble down the Niagara of fine sentiments and noble dreams. They have to be assigned a function and harnessed within the exchange system, for in no other way can the system shake of its fictitious fetters to move consistently towards its maximum.[16]

I have, in these two chapters twelve and thirteen, been pointing quite beyond the core generalization, for its full realization depends on that beyond, a beyond of a later stage of human meaning: certainly it can be called "the mature or the positive Anthropocene." But the beginnings here are a psychic stirring that would foster the suspicion that all is not well in the

---

[12] Regarding this central problem that hovers over future economics and politics, I would merely recall the obvious, that there is not some simple solution of taxation or bureaucracy or neat Marxist slogan, "to each according to whatever …" The phrase "unequal balance" above should leave you puzzled: it points you to the reality of humanity: "Men are unequal in ability and in opportunity." *For a New Political Economy*, 36. The solution to that problem is not "a Niagara of fine sentiments and noble dreams." *Ibid.*, and further quoted in the text below. It is a massive generalization, a science of the positive Anthropocene, and on that same 1942 page Lonergan wrote that "to determine the nature of such a generalization is the aim of this inquiry."

[13] Greek for 'measure.'

[14] My little book points to Lonergan in an elementary fashion, but the pointing includes us getting a grip on its unfinished character, our unfinished characters. "The treatment of character is a branch and starting point of statement" (Aristotle, paragraph 1 of *Magna Moralia*: quoted fully at note 11 on page 139), and wow do our characters need treatment!

[15] This is a very complex topic: briefly, living in a world of initial meanings is common sense ravaging humanity with colorful nominalism.

[16] Lonergan, *For a New Political Economy*, 36.

science and practice of present economics, that indeed there is at present no science of economics at all.

In chapter six at note 6 (p. 32) I looked ahead to the fantasy of a strange world of a high civilization of gardening, and one might well follow that fantasy in a weave of synaesthetics far beyond such glimmerings of "the music of the spheres"[17] as C. S. Lewis had in mind in writing *Perelandra*. But the start is a small molecular stirring in and by your whattage, your what-edge. That is, for you and for history, the "one condition."[18] Are you there yet? Certainly, as a polis and town—reach around in sniffed ugliness[19]—we are not there yet. Perhaps my concluding here with the vigorous plea of Bernard Lonergan in 1942 might twirl behind your eyes to seed a sense that, yes, you have been massively misled about what "abstract concepts"[20] are, and so massively misled about the joyous fermenting of sunflowers and butterflies of your molecular mind. Then you can read with me freshly the seeming stale claim in the next sentence about the "ooze of abnormality"[21] of our culture as it blocks the joy of minding. "What is lacking is the cultural milieu habituated to the use of abstract concepts and trained in the techniques that guard their employment."[22]

So I cannot now resist the temptation, in halting this stage of my plea, to quote in a fulsome fashion from Lonergan's 1942 work that invites us to pause at more length over what is lacking. He had just been remarking on

---

[17] Shakespeare, *Pericles*, Act 5, scene 1, line 228.

[18] I am referring ahead of its occurrence to the second sentence of the quotation which ends this chapter. The notes that follow on the way there help you to climb, if you have time, if you make time, caught in the slime, an Anthropocene slime.

[19] Feeling the slime grime your heart is just as remote an achievement as weaving into the molecular sublime of music's call, caul.

[20] Here, hear, the heart might ache in the caul of music for the genuine mindmeld in and with abstract concepts which are what-abstracted behind the ayes even of slime. The abstract addition is spirit's glimpse of the universe, "the concept emerges from understanding, not an isolated atom detached from all contexts, but precisely as part of a context" (Lonergan, *Verbum: Word and Idea in Aquinas*, ed. Frederick Crowe and Robert Doran, vol. 2, *Collected Works of Bernard Lonergan* [Toronto: University of Toronto Press, 1997], 238), with neighborhood's atoms lit up. Might we make a beginning on rescuing the little word "abstract" in the next chapter, sniffing a core cop-on to healing ourselves and history? The deep issue is our native meaning of context.

[21] Lonergan, *Insight*, 262.

[22] *Ibid.*, 559.

remote possibilities of financing the emergence of a global civilization, the remark quoted at note 6, page 32.

But we are not there yet. And for society to progress towards that or any other goal it must fulfill one condition. It cannot be a titanothore, a beast with a three-ton body and a ten-ounce brain. It must not direct its main effort to the ordinary final product of standard of living but to the overhead final product of cultural implements. It must not glory in its widening, in adding industry to industry, and in feeding the soul of man with an abundant demand for labor. It must glory in its deepening, in the pure deepening that adds to aggregate leisure, to liberate many entirely and all increasingly to the field of cultural activities. It must not boast of science on the ground that science fills its belly. It must not glue its nose to the single track of this or that department. It must lift its eyes more and ever more to the more general and more difficult fields of speculation, for it is from them that it has to derive the delicate compound of unity and freedom in which alone progress can be born, struggle, and win through. Unity without freedom is easy: set up a dictator and give him secret police. Freedom without unity is easy: let every weed glory in the sunshine of stupid adulation. But unity and freedom together, that is the problem. It demands discipline of mind and will: a keenness of apprehension that is not tied down to this or that provincial routine of familiar ideas nor yet has sunk to the jellyfish amorphism of skepticism; a vitality of response to situations that can acknowledge when the old game is done for, that can sacrifice the perquisites of past achievement, that can begin anew without bitterness, that can contribute without anticipating dividends to self-love and self-aggrandizement. The point is evident: a bureaucracy can imitate but it cannot create, for the spirit bloweth where it listeth, and all new ideas are ridiculous until the contrary is demonstrated by individual initiative, adapted by creative imagination, carried through by personal risk. Chaos can create, but it creates anything at all; it thinks of poison gas as well as anesthetics, and it uses both; it devises financial mechanisms that float brilliant booms and suffer incomprehensible slumps; it builds the wealth of cities and their slums; it inveighs against evil but it has to throw all civilization into the pot of experiment before it can discover whether another novelty will merit a blessing or a curse; it debauches the mind with a Babel of contradictions and leaves the will prey to fantasy and fanaticism.

To conclude: all the functions of the primary and the secondary rhythms are integral to the universal process. That consists not merely in widening, in deepening for more widening, and both for cheap pleasures and amusements. The cultural overhead and the deepening that releases man to leisure and culture are also essential parts—parts too easily overlooked—in the world rhythm of economic transformations. Nor will it suffice to have some highest common factor of culture, to accept the physical sciences but not bother about their higher integration on the plea that that is too difficult, too obscure, too unsettled, too remote. That was titanathore's attitude to brain, and titanothore is extinct.[23]

---

[23] Lonergan, *For a New Political Economy*, 20–21.

14

COMPLAINTS, COPON AND PROFIT III

A spectre is haunting Economics—the spectre of complaint. All the powers of the old Economics have entered into a holy alliance to exorcise this spectre: Pope and Tsar, Meternich and Guizot, French radicals and German policemen.[1]

I am returning, at the end of this Part Three, to the twist on Marx's beginning of the *Communist Manifesto* that I gave in the Preface. In that first sentence Marx has the word *communism*, not *complaint*. Yet is there not a sense in which a great deal of contemporary complaint and protest is an appeal for some brand of communism, commonness? So I recall a previous effort to invite a beginning of an economics that would be also a beginning of the positive Anthropocene age, an essay titled "Teaching High School Economics: A Common Quest Manifesto."[2] Since 1984—I was not thinking of Orwell as I wrote this, but you now might well do so: Big Brother is not only watching, he's screwing your neurons—it has been clear to me that the break-through of cultural faculties would have its beginning in economics.[3] It has become clear to me since then that the focus of the revolution might well be in high school and undergraduate economics. But so far my plea and my perspective stand as ineffective complaints. It is just one of my complaints, a skimpy list of which will emerge at the end of chapter sixteen. But pause here and think, indeed, of the spectrum and spectre of complaints that haunt our entry into the third millennium. Furthermore, think of them in their consistent ineffectiveness, be they small or great: protests about the death of a Syrian child on the shore of the

---

[1] See this as presented in the Preface, at page iv.

[2] This is the title of *Prehumous* 1. This series of twelve essays is available at: http://www.philipmcshane.org/prehumous.

[3] I made the point in December 1984 in an article honoring what would have been Lonergan's 80th birthday of that month. The article is available in *Cantower* XXXIII, "Lonergan and Axial Bridges" (December, 2004), in the second section, pp. 7–20. The point is made at note 29. This *Cantower* essay as well as the rest of the series is available at: http://www.philipmcshane.org/cantowers.

Mediterranean or about the death of the rivers of Asia emerging from Tibet.[4] And then there are complaints about Israel.[5] In chapter sixteen we shall turn to muse over what I call micro-effective successes. Here I wish to look into a future, perhaps still a millennium or so away in identifiable structures, when the global faculties of culture enjoy a Bell-curve statistics of success, rather than some Poisson curve weaving round rare events.

I am adverting here to the key feature of futurology as a culture: the repetitive evolutionary dynamics that I associate with Oparin and Lonergan.[6] Complaint, in that later culture, is to be meshed, by cyclical effective care, into a vortex of patterns of self-luminous kindliness that reach into that global culture. It is as well to repeat here the structure presented earlier in this third part of the book,[7] a display of words that helps us to think concretely of what we feebly imagine.

capacity	cooperation	particular good
developed skills	institution	good of order
liberty	personal relations	terminal value

The center of the display, rather neatly, can hold our attention as the center, the axis, of this post-axial culture. It is to be a whirl, a spiral, of

---

[4] See Michael Buckley, *Meltdown in Tibet: China's Reckless Destruction of Ecosystems from the Highlands of Tibet to the Deltas of Asia* (New York: Palgrave Macmillan, 2014).

[5] The international mood of such complaints is finally growing, but the United States' role in the last fifty years is beyond disgraceful by any simple standard of decency. I find myself in outraged agreement with Noam Chomsky's well-documented stand in his writings, lectures, and interviews.

[6] This points to the hope at the heart of this little book, densely introduced in chapter twelve. It pivots on the statistical significance of recurrence patterns, be it in chemicals or in cultures. A broad context is given in my early book, *Randomness, Statistics and Emergence* (Macmillan and University of Notre Dame Presses, 1970). See there, on Oparin, pp. 218–9, 225, 256. The point is made with heuristic precision by Lonergan on page 144 of *Insight*. Future studies will fill out this statistics in the case of the massive shift from negative to positive Anthropocene. But the effectiveness is to be a vortex movement of carers, carers who eventually will be perhaps in the region of a quarter of a billion people in a population of ten billion by the tenth millennium. See "Arriving in Cosmopolis," available at: http://www.philipmcshane.org/website-articles.

[7] See page 87.

collaborations, that is to continually, magnetically,[8] lift the global pattern of capacities—from *mewling* to the appearance of *sans everything*,[9] to ever-fresher patterns of micro-autonomy and liberty. Each complaint regards some "messy situation"[10] "headed for disaster."[11] Is there a remedy proposed or is it the case that "the messy situation is diagnosed differently by a divided community,"[12] so that "the situation becomes still messier to provoke still sharper differences in diagnosis and policy."[13]

Let us say that the diagnosis and policy is fitting, a stand against alienation. Then if it is not effective, it points to a failure in diagnosis and/or policy. That failure needs to be remedied. Can it, might it, be remedied within the situation, by communications and negotiations within the situation at the level of culture of the place and time? Then there occurs local progress, a progress which in reality is glocal progress. It is the remedying of the situation within the situation room, a remedying that we may call *COPON*. We met this remedy already, in note 3 of page 98, where I claimed that "future education is to be dominated luminously and self-luminously by the COPON Principle: 'When teaching children geometry, one is teaching children children.'"

Now COPON has been my topic from the beginning, and you might well ask, even at this late stage, "Just what have we been at, just what is COPON?"

And I am so glad you asked, although the answer is there in a jumble of your four words: COPON is just what, COPON is *Das Jus Was*.[14] There?

---

[8] Recall Pound's Vorticism introduced at the conclusion of chapter twelve, at note 17. I am simply adding dynamic images to the explanatory heuristics to which I pointed in note 6. And it is worthwhile for you to let your imagination take straining flight on seeming impossibilities. For instance the word *kindliness* was used in the text just above this note. Imagine the climb out of the accepted meanness of public life to—is it an oxymoron?—a globe of political kindliness. This should give a lift to your reading of other texts here on kindliness or mildness of manner: see the text at note 11 of page 81, or note 8 (p. 138) of the Epilogue.

[9] Shakespeare, *As You Like It*, II. 7. 143–166: early and late words—italicized by me—of his familiar seven stages of human life.

[10] Lonergan, *Method in Theology*, 358.

[11] *Ibid.*

[12] *Ibid.*

[13] *Ibid.*

[14] *Was? Dasein: und so weiter.* I twist you towards the German search associated with Heidegger. You might twist towards your own language and find, mind, your noises for searching, loneliness, being there, being wildered.

Dasein? But not yet there, luminously, in your neurodynamics. To get there it needs neurochemicals shaken up by images that stir the pot-ential whatwork. Let's try two simple leads into both COPON and the new economics.

A little puzzling, then, about a circle of unit radius in which you draw two diameters perpendicular to each other. From an arbitrary point P on the circumference two perpendiculars are drawn to the two diameters. The problem is, "What is the ratio of RS to the radius?" You have now drawn the figure? Perhaps even solved easily the puzzle? Your reaction to the puzzle and your solution of it will depend very much on your habit of mathematics. If mathematics leaves you cold, then you may find it hard enough to make a proper diagram much less solve the puzzle. If you are a mathematician then the solution is just too obvious. If you fall in between these two extremes then you may draw and mark and puzzle, even try trigonometry. Joining R and S will be an evident thing to do; but it may take a pedagogue to adequately fix the image by the drawing of another line. The line to draw is the line joining the center to the point, P, say, OP. Eureka! With the insight emerges the solution, the relation between RS and the radius.

Now note that the solution can be formulated or thrown into syllogistic form, and this will help you to get some light on features of the syllogism which are often misrepresented. We have, therefore, the syllogism:

$$RS = OP$$
$$\text{and} \quad OP = Radius;$$
$$\text{therefore} \quad RS = Radius.$$

In this light I may note important characteristics of procedure. We started, not with premises, but with the conclusion in the form: RS ? Radius. Our search, through diagram, was for a middle term, and the middle term was supplied as soon as we adverted to the significance of OP. Only then can the syllogism be constructed: one might say that the insight is crystallized into a syllogism.[15]

---

[15] You can find this page of the text in a useful elementary context on page 67 of *Wealth of Self and Wealth of Nations: Self-Axis of the Great Ascent* (Washington, DC: University Press of America, 1975). This book is available online at: http://www.philipmcshane.org/published-books.

The second puzzling opportunity is simply presented: a matter of splitting the alphabet in two, thus:

A   E F . . . .
   B C D

I start the split: can you finish it, replacing the dots with the other 20 letters? You need to figure out why the "ups and downs." In sixty years of presenting it to all types I have found professors extraordinarily slow, children sometimes embarrassingly swift![16]

The two puzzles together can help our struggle towards the new economics. Take the second "ups and downs" puzzle. The problem is to find out why. The deeper problem is to find out that finding out may take more time and energy than we expected. Think, then, of the ups and downs of the economy, or ups and downs of a friend's moods. Why, why, why? In the case of the economy's ups and downs one needs to get into the puzzle that parallels the circle puzzle. What is the relation of RS to the radius? Let's think of rising industrial activity, so RS points conveniently to Rising Surplus,[17] and then consider the radius as related to a norm of circulation of consumer goods.

So we have RS ? Radius. Or have we? Have we, had you, been had by ?? The professors of economics certainly have not had that serious ?. What is the answer? We are back in chapter two, trying to add crossover lines, G' and G". Why are there ups and downs in the dynamics of a creative economy? Because there are natural oscillations of the crossovers, the investment flow, the consumer-bent flow.

In all these cases and illustrations we are dealing with, living in, the sequence of networked global situations that form history. The challenge of the post-axial Anthropocene Age is to have a central luminous existential presence at the heart, knocking at the heart, of the global community

---

[16] I recall various amusing experiences that you may find consoling. There was the sociology professor with whom I doodled for two hours before she got the point; there was the six-year old who wandered up to a puzzling session with her parent and got the point in that embarrassing swiftness.

[17] Rising Surplus? You begin to glimpse this, perhaps, in the case of the plough invention of chapter three or even in the global cases pointed to in chapters seven and eight? I make no attempt in this little book to deal with the varieties of its oscillations, even in the simple case. For that simple case, see Lonergan's discussion in *For a New Political Economy*, 274–84.

regarding and guarding that living. It is to be the core, the luminous core, the *cor*, the heart, the mollyheartbeat, of every standard of living.

Cast your eyes now back to the display of nine words a few pages back and leap to a fantasy of their meaning-to-come.[18] It helps in that fantasy to lift the vortex meaning of COPON into that wisp of fantasy.

We have paused over an initial meaning, a copon to copon: the pausing is a wish to cranial-seed, wishing you to suck-seed: if you have the nerve[19] to attend to what your what is doing. Might you extend your attention to others in their copons, to all copons and copoffs, to the total story of what in a crazy anticipation of a global cyclic cyclic cyclic science of what care? A science of copon to copon to copon everywhere, an open heart surgering of anamnesis and prolepsis to make America globally great, grating on graft and craft the world over? A science of finding and fostering COPON's center, which is promise, the profit announced by the Profi-tearing Jeremiah,[20] a

---

[18] The key shift is to be towards a common meaning global meaning of the central **institution** of global progress, the situational dynamics that was the topic of chapter thirteen.

[19] To have the nerve: that was the issue raised in my peculiar way of pointing at the critical faculty of culture in chapter thirteen.

[20] My curious twisted expression as I introduce Jeremiah here points you to the world that I have kept to the side in this little book. Am I not only playing Plato to Dionysius, but also Jeremiah to the Hebrew-Christian tribes? I am certainly talking, in both cases, about a law written in hearts (*Jeremiah* 31:33). Reading the law fully, however, is a giant task beyond the central nudging of this little book. Think, now, of the climb involved in rising above the stench of the Israel-U.S. alliance mentioned in note 5 above. One might think of it, certainly, as an alliance involving Jews and Christians. That thinking can be put in the context of our slim musings in this chapter about COPON by a simple leap to the form of the puzzle of the circle above at note 16 above. Leap with me to replace "the form: RS ? Radius" a few lines above the footnoting there (p. 108), to the form OT ? NT. So we are back, or forward, to looking for a middle term, but a middle term that is not pivoting on an "=" but on some broader form of containment in the circle of humanity: a larger logic. What might that middle term be? It is no longer a matter of simple geometry but concrete history, indeed as it is to be reached for slowly in the circle of functional collaboration briefly named in chapter twelve. Part of the struggle to that distant context is a fresh reading of OT and NT: might I nudge you to that reading by writing *Old Tom* and *N.T.*? That writing lets me drop the "?" in "OT ? NT" for I am naming the same man: Nicholas Thomas Wright is also known as Tom: the outstanding biblical scholar. I have written critically of him elsewhere (see the *Disputing Quests* 4 and 5, "Studying Scripture: Turn Wright" (available at: http://www.philipmcshane.org/disputing-quests), but his grip on

new plough sifting from Gaia gifts for all, "from each according to his ability, to each according to his needs."[21]

So I return to a further brief nudge about the meaning of profit and the origin of its new meaning. Bernard Lonergan's third chapter of his 1942 version has the title "Transition to Exchange Economy."[22] The chapter is part of our communal climb to the new meaning of profit. But the 38-year-old had not broken forward to the full character of the transition; nor did he have the energy in his last years to lift his meaning to positive Anthropocene heights.[23] He pushed on to convey that the new meaning would involve an

---

initial meanings of that story is quite unique, expressed in about sixty books. Where might we begin our puzzling towards COPON here? In one of his many unpublished talks, he suggested to his audience, as I suggest to you now, "read *Isaiah*, chapters 40–55 in one serious sitting," and thus find your poise, or your absent poise. I bluntly suggest now that both traditions involved have lost the meaning of the story. "How can you insist, Israel, 'My destiny is hidden from Yahweh, my rights are ignored by my God'? Did you not know? Had you not heard?" *Isaiah*, 40: 27-28. "Yes, you will leave with joy and be led away in safety. Mountains and hills will break into joyful cries before you and all the trees of the countryside clap their hands." *Isaiah*, 55:12.

[21] The heuristic push, used by Marx, was first used by Louis Blanc in 1851, but its roots are in the 1755 Code of Nature of the French communist Morelly. Thinking it out empirically "is a vast task" (*For a New Political Economy*, 105: 6th last line) of the move to a positive Anthropocene Age. Then there is the vast task for you of this little book that, yes, can be put in the same form as the Israel problem of the previous note. Here you have a neat identification of the problem that I have kept dangling annoyingly before you all the way through: FE ? TE. "From each", "to each": what is the connection? Our full problem is to find concretely the massive middle term, a story-changer. You move to finding the central clue by pondering on such things as the 3rd chapter island-sharing after Joey's bright idea. Here you are looking for a bright idea absent from present economics and politics, "for on that precise topic it has no ideas whatever." *For a New Political Economy*, 298. My final nudge comes in the final note of the Epilogue, note 15 on page 141. But you might well get cauled into the climb—that would be jus' Kapital!—through musing on the two final footnotes here: notes 24 and 25 (p. 112).

[22] The title of chapter 3 of *For a New Political Economy*, *CWL* 21, 28-41.

[23] This is an altogether too difficult topic to get into here. Think of the gap between his meaning of *transition* in that chapter title of 1942 and his meaning of 25 years later that led me to think out the shift, the transition, involved in the positive Anthropocene Age.

intussusception of the meaning "social dividend"[24] lurking in the Marxian adage that ends the previous paragraph. It would have been a slight shift for him to begin to talk of "a global dividend." But it is up to us, in this millennium, to lift that talk into global nerves and hearts in a full dynamics of luminous promise.[25]

---

[24] Profit I, II, and now III, leave you obscure on the answer to the fundamental question of the book. Surely you did not expect some leap to clarity? Recall my chat in chapter five about summaries. But here you have a name: the clear operative conception of *social dividend* as the solution to the problem. Have you found some clues to it as you puttered along with me? I add some "definitional talk" from Lonergan to your obscure 'basic human longing' (see Fukayama below). "The basic mistaken expectation rests on a failure to distinguish between normal profit which can be constant, and a social dividend which varies." *Macroeconomic Dynamics*, 81. The social dividend is "income over and above 'standard of living,' 'rent,' interest, maintenance and replacement of capital equipment"; it is a "means given to entrepreneurs, investors, because they are the most likely to be able to interpret what it is for, namely, the successful introduction into the economic process of technological, commercial, or organizational improvements." *Ibid.*, 133, note 186. Profit IV, weaved around these nudges, will point us towards the distant center of the positive Anthropocene, way beyond the ridiculous view of such as Francis Fukayama, who suggests that we find the end of history in liberal democracy and consumerism, etc., a regime that best "satisfies the most basic human longings." Francis Fukayama, "Reflections on *The End of History*, Five Years Later," in *After History? Francis Fukuyama and His Critics*, ed. Timothy Burns (Lanham, MD: Rowman & Littlefield, 1994), 241. Against such nonsense do we not stand, if only in fantasy: our constitutions, our characters, our basic longings, secretly reaching for Amendment **A**? (introduced at footnote 2 of chapter eleven: p. 85).

[25] Might I not end this Part Three on a high note, pointing to a name, *promise*, as the Greeks used the name *element* in identifying 4 elements, an identification vastly distant from the identification of elements given by quantum chemistry. My meaning of *promise* is altogether more remotely distant from the meaning to which we must needs climb. Money is a promise, but what do we mean by *promise*? We mean, 99% of us, nothing more than an initial meaning, even if at times it is rich with feeling. Its full meaning is to lift self-interest and self-control into global promise: and what is that? Lonergan ends the first-page "Outline of the Argument" of his 1944 essay on economics with talk of the needed leap away from Keynes' nominalism of self-interest continued in our brutal and stupid times: "The exchange economy is confronted with the dilemma either of eliminating itself by suppressing the freedom of exchange or of certain classes of exchanges, or else of effectively augmenting the enlightenment of the enlightened self-interest that guides exchanges." *For a New Political Economy*, 232. The core crisis in the middle

daze of the negative Anthropocene Age is to tackle the task of effectively discovering the self-meaning of self-control. Meeting that crisis is at the heart of the "vast task" Lonergan wrote of at the end of his 1942 economic essay. For further guidelines see *Disputing Quests* 7: "Self-Control in the New Testament and in the Economics of the Positive Anthropocene Age," available at: http://www.philipmcshane.org/disputing-quests.

PART FOUR

2020 VISION

15

PIKETTY'S DARK MONEY

We return in these final three chapters to the reality of today and these next four years. Are we returning to *Realpolitik*? We must distinguish. If by that is meant that I am moving out of the perspective suggested in the previous Part Three, or trying to tailor suggestions about an effective meaning of profit to a clean-up of the Black or Grey Money traditions, or to rescue Piketty's shaky search for a new economics, or to show how Trump's odd view of taxing heads us in a usual destructive direction, or to consider flushing out the idiot manner in which elected officials of government spend a third of their office time fishing for other colors of money, etc., etc.: the answer is no.

The reforms I am looking to and for, amid the grey goings-on of government officials and lobbyists, are not the expected ones regarding Wall Street, or Health Care, or security, or wages, or climate, or whatever. Dark money, Pharma power, fracking, gun-toting, etc., etc., will be around long after Trump's reign and replacement. The reforms I am looking for would be way out of character for Donald, but I might well annoy him or those hostile to him to attend to them. The trickle down and up and round effectiveness I am looking for is a massive structure-lifting shift from economic voodoo to economic science by 2020—or 2050—that may well only be seeded by then in some strange group of serious economists who see beyond the biases of an Oval Office, erroneous economics, idiot lobbyists. Who owns Donald Trump's carpet? Perhaps he owns more of it than the previous president did. But that leaves him brutally grounded.

I am thinking here back to Obama's first inaugural address, when he said:

> "cynics fail to understand that the ground has shifted beneath them, that the stale political arguments that have consumed us for so long no longer apply." The sentiment was laudable but alas, wishful thinking. Had the newly sworn-in president looked down at the ground directly beneath his polished shoes as he delivered these optimistic words, he might have been wise to take note. The red-and-blue carpet on which he was standing, which had been custom made in accordance with a government contract, had

been manufactured by Invista, a subsidiary of Koch industries. In American politics, the Kochs and all they stood for were not so easy to escape.[1]

So ends Mayer's Introduction, "The Investors," which focuses on the Koch outrage at Obama's election and the Koch seminars' consequent drive against reform. My chapter heading here suggests a merging of the two books, Mayer's and Piketty's, in the drive towards elements of reform, and I might well have given book-length attention to Mayer as I did to Piketty.[2] Here I wish only for some effective disturbing attention to education, and in particular to economic education. I invite you to think of situations of failed education that, perhaps, impinge on you. There is, for instance, the Koch grip on economic education at Florida State University where

> the Koch influence was nefarious and omnipresent. Jerry Funt, an undergraduate, said that in the public university's introductory course, 'We learned that Keynes was bad, the free market was better, that sweatshops labor wasn't so bad, that the hands-off

---

[1] Jane Mayer, *Dark Money*, 22–23.

[2] The focus, of course, would be different, weaving round both dark philanthropy and law rather than economics. Think, for instance, of the *Citizens United* decision. But Piketty's suggestions must be taken seriously in envisaging the climb beyond. "In his State of the Union address, Obama made headlines by denouncing the Court's decision, saying it 'was a reversal of a century of law that I believe will open the floodgates for special interests—including foreign corporations—to spend without limit in our elections.' In response, the associate Supreme Court justice Samuel Alito Jr., who attended the address, was seen shaking his head and mouthing the words 'not true.'" *Dark Money*, 239. Tackling warped law and dark philanthropy, and "the pathological pursuit of profit and power" (the subtitle of Joel Bakan's book, *The Corporation*), requires a slow intussusception into culture of the taxing suggestions of Piketty within an equally slow-growing of effective new economics. The pathology must come to be recognized as such—recall the focus of chapter thirteen—so that there emerges an increasing autonomy in the rejection of the simple inhumanity of self-interested neurotic accumulation. Then there are the legal shifts regarding the madness of commodity money that need to come about, and the cultural displacement—e.g. in news casting—of the casino activities. All this is "a vast task. It means thinking out afresh our ideas of markets, prices, international trade, investment, return on capital. Above all, it means thinking out afresh our ideas on economic directives and control." (I quote from the concluding comments in Lonergan's analysis of 1942: *For a New Political Economy*, 105). This note lays all that aside, to let the text move on to pointing towards a single beginning zone in the vast task.

regulations in China were better than those in the U.S.' and 'climate change wasn't caused by humans and isn't a big issue. [3]

What did Jerry do?

What are you to do, whether or not you are Donald or Roy or Jane or Mervyn or Ian?

My focus here is on inviting you, yes, to muse as best you can on the new economics that emerges from the admission of the relevance of the two-flow analysis simply presented in chapters two and three. But the nudge goes further, Donald or Roy or Jane or Mervyn or Doe or Dear You. We need, for example, a shift in journalistic outreach to aid a shift in the culture of undergraduate economic education. We have to "get at" beginners in economics and its applications.[4]

So, among all the possible quests and questions upon which I might focus in this beginning of my final part, it seems best for me to home in on one. It is the question that bubbles up from Jerry Funt's situation. The question I would pose to you, to all facets of journalism, heavens even to economics professors: or perhaps you can pose it to them bluntly, for I have found them a very entrenched group . . . The question is, "Who owns the economics departments of universities?"

Obviously here I am venturing, not into the sociology of knowledge, or Kuhn's territory, but into journalistic nudgings. But my nudgings can make you think in that context, and yes, the ownership of tradition, be it as broad as fossil Marxism or fossil Capitalism, or as narrow as the usual fixity of a university department. There is also the fixity of a group establishment such as put paid to the suggestive little text of Joan Robinson and John Eatwell.[5] Bernard Lonergan, in his last years, began to reach around towards writing and publishing an introductory text: who would it have reached? My

---

[3] *Dark Money*, 365. The class's economics textbook "was co-written by Russell Sobel, the former recipient of Koch funding at West Virginia University who taught that safety regulations hurt coal miners." *Ibid.*

[4] We, of course, are among the beginners, but we have a responsibility in our stumblings to attend to the mess being handed on in our schools. I have various school texts to hand that are representative of the abomination, but perhaps I might restrict myself to referencing the child abuse in my native land: Denis L. O. Grady, *Leaving Certificate Economics* (Dublin: Follens, 2002).

[5] I have mentioned the text before, but best refer to it in the context of its rejection here. The text: *An Introduction to Modern Economics* (New York: McGraw Hill, 1973). Its rejection: see, in particular, Marjorie Turner, *Joan Robinson and the Americans* (Armonk, NY: M.E. Sharpe, 1990), 175–79.

own lecturing rambles round the globe bore no serious fruit, indeed they bore witness to shocking fixity. One chairperson in economics got the light, but admitted to me that nothing could be done: the department would teach the usual junk.

And what, you are possibly asking now, might get you to move to journalistic objection if not outrage? A year ago I took time to move through course outlines of various North American universities, and I built my outrage into the third chapter, "The Canons of Economic Meaning," of *The Allure of the Compelling Genius of History*.[6] There are six solid canons of serious inquiry. I restricted myself to the shocking fact that the inquiries of economic departments were slimly and erroneously empirical in betraying the first canon. Should I add a sample or three of outlines?

ECON 1102
Introduction to Macroeconomics
An introduction to the national macro-economy and the determinants of economic aggregates such as Gross Domestic Product (GDP), national income accounts, employment, and the price level. The government use of fiscal and monetary policies and the effects of these policies on economic variables will also be studied.

ECON 2201
Intermediate Macroeconomic Theory
Prerequisite: ECON 1102
The study of the determination of broad economic aggregates such as GNP, employment and the price level, analysis of problems such as inflation, unemployment, business cycles, economic growth and international financial crisis, and how governments respond to them.

ECON 2202
Intermediate Macroeconomics
Prerequisite: ECON 2201
A course designed to enable students to apply macroeconomic tools to analyze and solve empirical problems. The topics covered may include Keynesian, monetarist and supply-side theories and policies; econometric macromodels as vehicles for empirical analysis, forecasting and policy evaluation; and problems of the open economy.

---

[6] I weaved the chapter round the larger chapter three of Lonergan's *Insight*: "The Canons of Empirical Inquiry."

I see no point in adding comments on this standard diet of unfortunate students. Do you not smell stale unempirical palaver? But perhaps you are the student well and subtly prepared for this brain washing? Who owns your minding? Who owns the students? Do they not take seriously the economics sections of daily newspapers, which have altogether more to do with the second hand trade than with genuine economic goings-on? And to firm up their neurodynamic entrapment, there is the evening news which adds, to its repetitive ramble round global tragedies, the idiocy of stock market fluctuations. And, as the old joke has it, fluctueuropeans too!

16

MARX'S LIST

I recall now my preface forecast, one that relates to Marx's list, but in a quite fresh explanatory sense: "my vamp is to be not only beguilingly sexy but—yes—to eventually be successful. So, thinking of these objecting crowds, of marches against institutions of finance and government, of daily groanings in town and gown, I am led to give a twist to the first words of Marx's *Communist Manifesto*, replacing *Europe* with *economics* and *communism* with *complaint*: 'A spectre is haunting Economics—the spectre of complaint. All the powers of the old Economics have entered into a holy alliance to exorcise this spectre: Pope and Tsar, Metternich and Guizot, French radicals and German policemen.'"[1]

I return, in concluding this chapter, to the list in the original sense. But my concern now is with the list, the tilt, the confusing, of both Marx and the allies or cousins of the Koch brothers. Let us, so to speak, go full tilt at the explanatory perspective, recalling first our spread of words,[2] boldfaced from now on in this chapter:

capacity	cooperation	particular good
developed skills	institution	good of order
liberty	personal relations	terminal value

We have paused over these words before, and you may recall points made then, but now perhaps do so with a more self-luminous suspicion that the nine words, "Let us go full tilt at the explanatory perspective" aim us freshly at the weaving, through a global effort, of the nine topics in the display into a distant culture. I can best identify that aim for you, an aim of a life, an ontic and phyletic aim, in your self-puzzling over your poise over the full-tilt invitation. It is best identified as a luminous awakening to the

---

[1] See above, the Preface, page iv.
[2] See chapter eleven, p. 87; chapter fourteen, p. 106.

what in you, the what you are. How is that luminous awakening to get underway in you?

In Ian Angus's title-words, we are "facing the anthropocene: fossil capitalism and the crisis of the earth system." But is Ian just a Marxist fossil? Certainly, like Marx, he can claim that he is not a Marxist: yet in his drive to a fresh socialism he shows the Marxist absence of serious tilt towards luminous awakening. Serious understanding of himself or of nature's economic rhythms are not for him. So, he is happy with Marx's list, a list that simply does not take seriously the need for understanding that is at present packaged by axial culture in the neurodynamics of **capacity**. That neurodynamics binds and blocks and biases[3] the full nine interweaved realities, so that there is only bogus **liberty**, bogus **personal relations**, and vague namings of **terminal values**. We are back, of course, at the beginning of our reflections on the faculty of culture, but with little added identifications of a way forward. Think now of the simple pragmatic suggestion of seeding a revolution in journalism: but if it is to become even a little plant—yes, plant even in the lobbying sense—it needs subtle cultivation if it is not to end up with a Marxian list.

> While there is progress and while its principle is **liberty**, there is also decline and its principle is bias. There is the minor premise of group bias, which tends to generate its own corrective. There is the major principle of general bias, and though it too generates its own corrective, it does so only by confronting human intelligence with the alternative of adopting a higher viewpoint or perishing. To ignore the fact of decline was the error of the old liberal views of automatic progress. The far more confusing error of Marx was to lump together both progress and the two principles of decline under the impressive name of dialectical materialism, to grasp that the minor principle of decline would

[3] The next quotation, at note 4, is a comment by Lonergan on Marx as he is caught in biases. What might I say about them? Notes 7, 9, and 11 of chapter ten talk about the difficulty of reaching humanly towards meaning in a sick culture (respectively, pp. 79, 80, 81). In chapter five I wrote of the problem of summary presentation. Group bias is, briefly, what it says. General bias? We live in millennia of it. As it happens, I have to hand the first volume of John Ralston Saul's philosophic trilogy, *Voltaire's Bastards: The Dictatorship of Reason in the West* (New York: Penguin, 1993). Might you use it to make you pause, groping to glimpse whether there is really much sign of reason in the West, whether the West is not locked in the negative Anthropocene by gross commonsense pretensions?

correct itself more rapidly through class war, and then to leap gaily to the sweeping conclusion that class war would accelerate progress.[4]

You may well find yourself—what a quaint non-finding!—agreeing with me in some mode of journalism. But you must ask, "What am I lumping together as I read?" Are you, perhaps part of the *Lumpenproletariat* named by Marx but nicely identified by Saul Bellow as the masses of contemporary voters?[5] You thus identify yourself discomfortingly as not serious about the lumping and humping that is the dull daze of capitalism as it tinkers forward or pretends to trickle down. You may be interested financially in grandchildren going to college, but beyond that—might you pause and muse[6]—is your journeying, alas, not somewhat journalistic? We are back, are we not, with another of my titles, that provided by Roy Scranton, *Learning to Die in the Anthropocene Age*. But, really, is there any learning involved: do we not, rather, like veterans, fade away after we have been medaled with?

Just as in the previous chapter I homed in on journalism as a home-stirring, so here I hope that we are lifting that appeal about journalism into a suspicion of its need—a seemingly impossible pressure—to tune heart-

---

[4] Bernard Lonergan, *Insight*, *CWL* 3, 260.

[5] I am thinking here of Ortega y Gasset's *The Revolt of the Masses* and note that Ortega's notion of the masses was quite complex. Chapters 6 and 8 of his book are directly on the topic, but also chapter 12 on "The Barbarism of Specialization." Saul Bellow, in his Foreword to the translation, neatly sums up Ortega and also the problem of the changes in the meaning of mass man since Ortega's time. "Ortega when he speaks of the mass man does not refer to the proletariat: he does not mean us to think of any social class whatever. To him the mass man is an altogether new human type. Lawyers in the courtroom, judges on the bench, surgeons bending over anaesthetized patients, international bankers, men of science, millionaires ... differ in no important respect from TV repair men, clerks in Army-Navy stores, municipal fire-inspectors, or bartenders. It is Ortega's view that we in the West live under a dictatorship of the common place." *The Revolt of the Masses*, translated by Anthony Kerrigan, edited by Kenneth Moore, with a Foreword by Saul Bellow (South Bend, IN: University of Notre Dame Press, 1985), p. ix.

[6] Stay, or climb into, the context suggested in the previous notes. One needs to be something of an outsider to sense how sick the modern journey through life is. I think of Hermine talking to Harry Haller in Hermann Hesse's *Steppenwolf*: "Ah Harry, we have to stumble through so much dirt and humbug before we reach home. And we have no one to guide us. Our only guide is our homesickness." *Ibid.*, 179.

loosely into its ontic and phyletic **capacity.**[7] **Liberty**, in our times, takes a turn in some of us towards hope in some New Age[8] of poise and/or pause that may or may not lift our **personal relations,** our **terminal values**. But the poise and pause that supports the cosmic promise is old old aged, molecules ordered by a Big Bang and by a deep Anthropic Principle[9] towards a neurodynamics vibrant with aesthetic contemplative communal delight.

The beating heart of that growing delight is to be an "Interior Lighthouse"[10] fostered within the set of situation rooms, a kataphatic poise towards global care. But it is a poise than can be taken seriously by anyone:

---

[7] As I struggled to end the appeal of this little book, I was haunted by the task of "not flogging a row of dead horses" but rather inviting a single focused start on "an integral transformation of the whole previous position," the institutional complex. The two references here, however, allow me to end with more than my whimpering about journalism and journeying. So I quote the full paragraph of those references: Lonergan's claim regarding our unknown future. "There remains a further question, namely, Are there other limitations of the exchange economy besides this inability to attain the maximum of satisfactions? Obviously there are, else the solution would not lie in generalization, in an integral transformation of the whole previous position. But I do not think that there is any need to flog a whole row of dead horses; a flick at a particularly nauseating one is good enough; indeed, a wink is as good as a nod. Still one point does deserve attention, and it is this. A generalization will postulate a transformation not only of the old guard and its abuses but also of the reformers and their reforms; it will move to a higher synthesis that eliminates at a stroke both the problem of wages and the complementary problem of trade unions; it will attack at once both the neglect of economic education and the blare of advertisements leading the economically uneducated by the nose; it will give new hope and vigor to local life, and it will undermine the opportunity for peculation corrupting central governments and party politics; it will retire the brain trust but it will make the practical economist as familiar a professional figure as the doctor, the lawyer, or the engineer; it will find a new basis both for finance and for foreign trade. The task will be vast, so vast that only the creative imagination of all individuals in all democracies will be able to construct at once the full conception and the full realization of the new order." *For a New Political Economy*, 36–37.

[8] In these past decades the interest in this, and in the Zen-related traditions, has grown considerably: one need only view the "New Age" zone in larger bookstores.

[9] On the Anthropic Principle, see note 3 of the following chapter, at p. 130.

[10] The title "Interior Lighthouse" is taken from the thirteenth essay in a series named *HOW*. It points to the transformation of all types of contemplation. The series is available at: http://www.philipmcshane.org/how.

it is a fundamental **capacity** that is to lift global common sense to the positive Anthropocene.

In conclusion, let me come back to Marx's other list and let me think of my own list of those who would resist my suggestion of this ghost of Lonergan's economics, a spectre haunting Economics. "All the powers of the old Economics have entered into a holy alliance to exorcise this spectre: Pope and Tsar, Metternich and Guizot, French radicals and German policemen.""[11] Dare I write my list? Certainly there is no problem with the first two being replaced by the Pope and Putin. No comment is needed regarding Putin, but perhaps listing the present Pope is a surprise. But why should it be? Despite the fact that he probably heard of Lonergan, a fellow Jesuit, he is in the same position as Donald regarding this economics. Might he not do something about this Vatican stupidity, this entrenched Vatican tilt?

Instead of French radicals and German policemen I find I have radical Lonergan scholars who herd off Lonergan and would police his simpler simplified suggestions to suit a non-revolutionary Christianity. What conservative politicians and historians are to replace Klemens von Metternich and Francois Guizot two centuries later? Check your own back yard, for they have been abundantly replaced: their bureaucrats crawl round in your life like robodrones, snuffing out global promise.

The spectre that is an inconvenience in all their tiny tiny lives is the spooky disturbing **capacity** at the heart of humanity that refuses[12] to settle for a habitat in a circus of work when its, your, rightful place is the catching universe caught in its, your, inner galactic delight.

---

[11] See above, the Preface, page iv.

[12] The refusal takes a myriad forms, from childhood wonder to X-Factor aspiration, but its roots are identifiable by you in so far as you take seriously the search hidden in the claim that we share sensitivity with the animals, "something we share with the higher animals but, while they live in a habitat, we live in a universe because we asks questions and our questions are unrestricted." Lonergan, "Horizons and Categories," *Early Works on Theological Method I* (Toronto: University of Toronto Press, 2010), *CWL* 22, 482: modified by me from 'he' to 'we'. On the dynamics and tensions of the human quest, see Lonergan, *Insight*, 469–79, 747–51. The latter reference carries us into the world described at the end of chapter fourteen above.

17

CLEARING THE AIR FOR THE HEIRS

> "I thought I saw the fallen flower
> Returning to its branch
> Only to find it was a butterfly."[1]

Thirty five years ago I took a year off to write a 23-page Preface to a book titled, *Searching for Cultural Foundations*. That Preface leaped at me as amazingly relevant to this appeal of mine, a final print-appeal this, at the age of 85. The title of that Preface is "Distant Probabilities of Persons Presently Going Home Together in Transcendental Method." The last two words can conveniently be replaced by the single capital word, "COPON," a word brooded on in chapter fourteen, "Complaints, COPON, and Profits III." The word has a simple slang meaning that I have pushed in this little book to become the heuristic sign of cosmic loneliness and longing: a gadfly sign, a butterfly word.

At all events, I was led by my musing on that previous effort to begin this final chapter with the *haiku* that began that Preface, and indeed to end this short chapter by using the final words of that Preface, thus bringing us back to the butterfly.

But what of the in-between of both pieces, where those two in-betweens are indeed poised over the in-between of history in which we now muddle along in shocking industrious destructiveness of a natural world that includes humanity?

The invitation of this little book is towards us, led by some evolutionary sports, finding our way out of this in-between, these axial centuries of overdrive and overreach and gross confusion about self-understanding. It is towards us learning to live and die in the Anthropocene, beyond the

---

[1] "Raka eda ni / Kaeru to mireba / Kocho Kana". The haiku is quoted from Laurens van der Post, *A Portrait of Japan* (New York: William Morris and Company, 1968), 107. This quotation begins my Preface, "Distant Probabilities of Persons Going Home Together in Transcendental Method," to *Searching for Cultural Foundations* (Lanham, MD: University Press of America, 1984).

anthropo-obscene. So I come to my promised[2] return to Roy Scranton, indeed to address Roy Scranton, as representing magnificently one of the groups on my list of the previous chapter. An Iraq veteran, he has burst forward out of successful journalism to a first book, *Learning to Die in the Anthropocene Age*.[3] Might I nudge him forward, beyond the obscenity he so well identifies, by pointing to the stupidity, the datedness, of his views on "the collapse of carbon-fueled capitalism"[4] and of "adapting, with mortal humility, to our new reality?"[5] Nor, in this claim, do I wish to take issue with his seeming reductionism, but accept positively his concluding assertions. "We are finite and limited machines, but we are not merely machines: we are vibrating bodies of energy, condensations of stellar dust and fire, at once matter and life, extension and thought, moment and frequency."[6] The Anthropocene, at its future finest,[7] will align itself with nature in meshing whats' full natural reaching with the reaching of the molecules of the first cosmic second.[8] But in the short term? I share his blunt pessimism: "We're fucked. The only questions are how soon and how badly."[9] Yet I share his quiet optimism, weaved round the humanities. "The fate of the humanities, as we confront the end of modern civilization, is the fate of humanity itself."[10] But, whereas he appeals to the story-telling of the humanities, I would have him and us weave that appeal into a creative genetics of those

---

[2] See above, note 7 of page iii and note 6 of page x.

[3] City Lights Books, 2015, referred to below as *Scranton*. On pages 17–18 he talks of the term *Anthropocene* as now a respected one for our age of effective human differentiating evolutionary progress. The fullest meaning of Anthropocene needs the context I gave it in *Lack in the Beingstalk* (Vancouver: Axial Publishing, 2006), where I pushed for refinements of the Anthropic Principle (*op. cit.*, 85–86).

[4] *Scranton*, 23.

[5] *Ibid.*

[6] *Ibid.*, 115.

[7] I have written in various places about expected patterns of refinement and progress, hovering over a period of history that begins with the tenth millennium. See "Arriving in Cosmopolis." The essay was originally a lecture of 2011 in Puebla, Mexico, so I focus on the date 9011 A.D., as I do later in the book *The Road to Religious Reality* (Vancouver: Axial Publishing, 2012). "Arriving in Cosmopolis" is available in both English and Spanish at: http://www.philipmcshane.org/website-articles.

[8] A context is the final sentence of page 722 of Lonergan's *Insight*: "Good will wills the order of the universe, and it so wills with that order's dynamic joy and zeal."

[9] *Scranton*, 16.

[10] *Ibid.*, 109.

stories that would lift what's what into freshly, futurologically, "attending to the historical and philological genealogies of our current conceptual symbolic structures of existence to recognize who we are, who we have been, and who we might become."[11] I note his reach here, and invite him, and other journalists, and indeed the messy world of academic humanities, to face the challenge of this new context:

> I've relied mainly on Greek examples, but the roots of our contemporary civilization are also Akkadian, Sumerian, Chinese, Indian, Mesoamerican, Judaic, Egyptian, Nubian, Thule, Dorset and Finno-Ugric. Anywhere humans live, we make meaning. The record of that wisdom, the heritage of the dead, is our most valuable gift to the future.[12]

The new context would have our global whatters place the messy ineffective interest, such as Scranton displays, into a global community effecting situations, oval offices and rectangular classrooms, spires and mine-shafts. This is a massive going beyond "Flood Wall Street, which began with a marching band, dancing, and speeches from Naomi Klein, Chris Hedges, Mamadou Goïta, Elisa Estronioli, and others."[13] The new flooding has to reach Main Street. I think of an old title of mine for the revolution, "A Rolling Stone Gathers *Nomos*," but now ask you to think of the fifty-year old magazine, *Rolling Stone*, lifted into that world, "Rolling Stone Gathers *Nomos*."[14] Now there is a nudge for it and all other media of comment and complaint. Nudge? Do I have to write to—or, better, about!—editors accusing them of having stupid views?

Have I twirled and twisted round my strategy sufficiently in this little book, or should I go further with *"fare lo stupido"*[15]—play the fool: even

---

[11] *Scranton*, 98.

[12] *Ibid.*, 99.

[13] *Ibid.*, 64.

[14] "A Rolling Stone Gathers Nomos" is the title of two chapters of two of my books: chapter five of *Economics for Everyone: Das Jus Kapital*, 2nd edition (Vancouver: Axial Publishing 1998). and chapter three of *A Brief History of Tongue: From Big Bang to Coloured Wholes* (Halifax: Axial Publishing, 1998). They both relate the "situation room" structure presented in chapter twelve above to the needs and directions, respectively, of economics and linguistics.

[15] I borrow the term from Bernard Lonergan, *Phenomenology and Logic*, edited by Philip McShane (Toronto: University of Toronto Press, 2001), 317. "In Italian churches one of the techniques they employ is to have a person who simulates great stupidity ask the questions that the preacher answers. It is known as *fare lo*

asking you, Donald or Roy or whomever, to play the fool? "You would want to do a good job of being the stupid fellow. You cannot avoid that tendency to ask *why*, to ask *what*."[16] Thus you would come to teeter on the edge of discovering your humanity and its stupid truncations in these later axial times. Most of us recognize that Donald accommodated in the autumn of 2016 to play the fool: what a 100 days of idiocy we had before November 8th!—but Roy is by no means playing the fool. Might he take me seriously and follow up his first merciless novel, *War Porn* (2016), with a struggle towards a seeding of cycles of *Peace Born*? Then his "Coming Home" would weave round my "going home," our home-seeking. So I end by paying lengthy respect to his vision.

> This astonishing cosmos is our home. There is no other. There is no Heaven, no Hell, no Judgment, no Elysium.[17] We humans are precocious multicellular energy machines building hives on a rock in space, machines made up of and connected to countless other machines, each of us a microcosm. Trillions and trillions of microorganisms live on our skins and in our stomachs, mouths, intestines, and respiratory tracts while we spin through our lives in innumerable intersecting orbits, shaped and pulled by forces beyond our reckoning. We are machines or machines in machines, all and each seeking homeostatic perpetuation, and our lives and deaths pass through this great cycle like mosquitos rising and falling in a puddle drying in the summer sun.[18]

But for me, the mosquito rising and falling is replaced by the leaf that is indeed a butterfly. The task of humanity, the humanities, is to pass, century by century, through the "great cycles" of Futurology that are to be Anthropocene's evolutionary core.

So, I butterfly-end by skipping from an end-leaf of his little book to the conclusion of my little Preface of thirty-five years ago.

---

stupido [to play the fool]. But if anyone of us were called upon to *fare lo stupido* we would want to do it in an intelligent way."

[16] *Ibid.*

[17] Problems lurking here are beyond this little effort of mine. They relate to the neurodynamic drives of humanity for aesthetic explanatory identity. The end chapters of my *The Allure of the Compelling Genius of History* (Vancouver: Axial Publishing, 2015) are a help.

[18] *Scranton*, 112.

Part of the glory of history is man's envisagement of its schedules of probabilities and possibilities. If the sapling of history is cut down within, still it can have, within, a vision of the temporal noosphere that, paradoxically, redeems God. The envisagement is the core of future academic growth: its opposite is an elderhood that is the fraud of being in reality 'not old folk but young people of eighteen, very much faded.'[19] Our molecules, 'our arms and legs filled with sleeping memories,'[20] passionately demand that we fly after the butterfly.

> 'There the butterfly flew
> away over the bright water,
> and the boy flew after it,
> hovering brightly and easily,
> flew happily through the blue space.
> The sun shone on his wings.
> He flew after the yellow
> and flew over the lake
> and over the high mountain,
> where God stood on a cloud
> and sang.'"[21]

---

[19] Marcel Proust, *Remembrance of Things Past* (New York: Random House, 1932), vol. 2, 1042.

[20] *Ibid.*, vol. 2, 874.

[21] Hermann Hesse, *Wandering*, translated by James Wright (New York: Farrar, Straus and Giroux, 1972), 89. This is quoted at the end of the Preface mentioned in note 1.

EPILOGUE

PROFIT IV

As I begin this Epilogue—an early sketching—at the end of August 2016, my native land is in the news. Apple, the European Commission says, owes Ireland thirteen billion Euros in back taxes. Ireland does not want it. America gets into the dispute. It will occupy many internationally during September and beyond, and parallels to the mess abound to make that 'beyond' something that prolongs the present horrors that belong to the negative beginnings of the Anthropocene age.

Even if I have something to say about Apple, and the Big Apple's Wall Street, and about the general financial global mess that comes from centuries of stupidity and cupidity, and about the American financing of Israel's crimes against the Palestinian people and about China's subtle out-reachings, and about Putin's kleptocracy, and about Africa's invasion by global meanness, and about Papal putterings, and about the world mirrored in Oliver Stone's film *Snowden*,[1] and so on and on and on: these are not my topic here. Dealing with them and with the global mess that crawls sickly and stickily round your grasses and graves and grins and groin—to pause over only a grrrr slice of the English dictionary of our lives—that is a task for the massive collaboration of the vortex of effective situation-room care of future millennia. A vast task. Not a task for sketching here, but a task way beyond my scattered hints in this little book. I am concerned with beginnings and with getting you similarly concerned. Similarly? Aye, there's the rub, the rub of a rolling stone gathering *nomos*. It is the rub of the hub of a seeding-wheel of a new creation, an invention of the wheel of the positive Anthropocene. I am again, but how freshly—"it's no use going back to yesterday because I

---

[1] I cannot resist, however, a final note here about whistleblowing. I doubt if Stone would be interested in a film about my whistleblowing. Yet, though it lacks romance, it reaches towards a far greater ill than Snowden's efforts. I am whistleblowing on a much deeper sickness than the CIA's evils. There is the evil of well-paid economics departments and their blind political hacks and their inhuman Wall Street exploiters maintaining a standard of misery the world over: a misery that subtly weaves global starvation and murder into its pathological antics.

was a different person then"[2]—back at my first chapter of *Economics for Everyone*, "Baskets and Handfills," and with the first sentence, borrowed from *An Introduction to Modern Economics*. "It is time to go back to the beginning and start again."[3]

Yet, am I not starting at the end? Certainly I am starting at the end of Bernard Lonergan's climb from the early 1930s to his first abrupt halt in 1942, when he sensed the need for a new beginning, some other way of seeding the vast task. But his ending is worth pausing over here: again, that word pausing which I—no doubt annoyingly—nudged you to pause over as I nudge you to pause. Still, some of you reading this get a sense of my twist, and my vortex, and my twisting hope to wind history towards the fullness of the Anthropocene age. The winding, again, is another vast task. Yet is it not the same vast task?[4] So let us pause over Lonergan's ending of his 1942 plea. Indeed as I look at that plea, with the intention of beginning freshly our pausing, at his talk of "a vast task,"[5] I see that it would be silly of me not to start at the beginning of his second last paragraph, a paragraph which ends his long section 49 on "The Financial Problem."[6] That section and that paragraph are followed by what I can call a gap, missing sections 50, 51, 52. Then he ends his effort with his bold—and boldfaced here—twenty-seven words under the heading "Mechanism of the Cultural Expansion": "**By a cultural expansion is meant a rate of increase in the production of overhead primary products, of the things by which civilization is defended, developed, maintained**." What primary products? Primary products of what? Primary products of what. And so we find our topic. But first, a double pause, as you'll find, over the previous paragraph, carrying forward there from talk of the invention of money and commodity money and laws of money and bookkeeping.

> On the other hand, when we say that the idea of money as a system of public bookkeeping has to be worked out and applied,

---

[2] Lewis Carroll, *Alice's Adventures in Wonderland*.

[3] Joan Robinson and John Eatwell, *An Introduction to Modern Economics* (New York: McGraw Hill, 1973), 52. (quoted at the beginning of chapter one of *Economics for Everyone: Das Jus Kapital*, 15)

[4] Have you by now your own answer to this? Think of the *Cosmopolis* required by Lonergan in *Insight*: "we do not hope to reach a full solution in this volume." *Insight*, 267. (For the section on Cosmopolis, see *Insight*, 263–67.) The structure emerges in the instituting of situation-room analysis.

[5] *For a New Political Economy*, 105.

[6] *Ibid.*, 100–106.

we mean above all the necessity of a money whose laws coincide with the laws of objective economic process, so that instead of conflict between real possibility and financial possibility we shall have harmony, and instead of bookkeepers exercising a dominant role they will fill a duly subordinated position. Thus, schematically, in the capitalist phase there will be a release of more money to give the DT" to the secondary circuit and to obtain for the redistribution area its necessary measure of liquidity; in the materialist phase there will be similar operations, and as well the need for a positive DC' to keep C' at unity will be explored; in the static phase the liquidity of the redistributional area will be reduced but the funds released along DC', DT', and DT" will not be recalled as though the idea of an expansion were a subsequent crash. Now to work out in detail the conditions under which this must be done, and to prescribe the rules that must be observed in doing it, is a vast task. It means thinking out afresh our ideas of markets, prices, international trade, investment, return on capital. Above all it means thinking out afresh our ideas of economic directives and controls. And if we are to do this, not on the facile model of the totalitarian or socialist regimes which simply seek to abolish the problems and with them human liberty, then there will be need not merely for sober and balanced speculation but also for all the concrete inventiveness, all the capacity for discovery and for adaptation, that we can command.[7]

And now I finally come out in the open, and Donald and all those whose stupidity I have complained of may breathe less fiery, and you, now reading, perhaps put puzzled impatience on hold regarding the question "What is profit?" For: answering is a vast post-axial task. The stupidity is an axial communality, the answer a begetting of an effective gripping. The effective answer is one that will carry us from the negative Anthropocene Age to the positive Anthropocene Age. And, yes, it is helpful to repeat those twenty-seven boldfaced words: **By a cultural expansion is meant a rate of increase in the production of overhead primary products, of the things by which civilization is defended, developed, maintained.**

---

[7] *Ibid.*, 105–106. The terminology here is different from that of his later work and from mine: but it is the impression of his post-Marxian control of meaning that is important here.

Overhead primary products? Primary products with growing COPON from kindergarten to post-grad?[8]

My book was obviously written during the American presidential campaign of 2016. Let us muse now over a campaign of fifty-six years ago, one that was closer to the reality of our global struggle than the autumn farce of the Clinton-Trump confrontations.

> A striking feature of the 1960 Presidential campaign was the emphasis by both candidates upon the importance of the Communist challenge to this country. Implicit in this was the concept of the importance that both men attached to a correct understanding of the system of ideas that we call Communism. Vice-President Nixon felt this understanding to be so important that one of his first major moves after being nominated was the issuance of a formal document assailing the prevalent general ignorance of Communism and seeking to give a brief exposition and critique of Communist ideas. At about the same time in the later summer of 1960, Central Intelligence Director Allen Dulles made a speech urging that education about Communism be included widely in the curricula of our schools.[9]

Let us add to that and to our context of puzzling over "What is profit?" a piece of Marx of the previous century:

> A fall in the rate of profit and a hastening of accumulation are in so far only different expressions of the same process as both of them indicate the development of the productive power. Accumulation in its turn hastens the fall of the rate of profit, inasmuch as it implies the concentration of labor on a large scale and thereby a higher composition of capital and its centralization

---

[8] I recall my optimism of thirty years ago. "If there is to be a massive shift in public minding and kindliness and discourse in the next century, there must be a proportionate shift in the mind and heart of the academy and the arts at the end of this century, with consequent changes in operating schemes of recurrence from government to kindergarten." Philip McShane, *Lonergan's Challenge to the University and the Economy*, 1976, 1. The book, a photocopy of Lonergan's copy, with his markings, is available at: http://www.philipmcshane.org/published-books. Now I think more in terms of the next millennium or seven rather than this century. But it is up to you! Recall note 8 (p. 107) of chapter fourteen.
[9] Harry Schwartz, "Introduction" to *Marx on Economics*, edited by Robert Freedman (New York: Harcourt, Brace and World, 1961), ix.

through the expropriation of the smaller capitalists, the expropriation of the last survivors of the direct producers who still have anything to give up. This accelerates on the one hand the accumulation, so far as mass is concerned, although the rate of accumulation falls with the profit. On the other hand, so far as the rate of self-expansion of the total capital, the rate of profit, is the incentive of capitalist production just as this self-expansion of capital is its only purpose, its fall checks the formation of new independent capitals and thus seems to threaten the process of the development of the process of capitalist production. It promotes overproduction, speculation, crises, surplus-capital along with surplus-population. Those economists who, like Ricardo, regard the capitalist mode of production as absolute, feel nevertheless, that this mode of production creates it own limits, and therefore they attribute this limit, not to production, but to nature (in their theory of rent). But the main point in their horror over the falling rate of profit is the feeling, that capitalist production meets in the development of productive forces a barrier, which has nothing to do with the production of wealth as such; and this peculiar barrier testifies to the finiteness and the historical, merely transitory character of capitalist production.[10]

Have we not still a problem of "a correct understanding of a system of ideas we call communism"—including oscillations in "the rate of profit"—that would mesh into the characters[11] of politics and the "curricula of our

---

[10] *Ibid.*, 202: quoting from Karl Marx, *Capital*, Volume III, Charles Kerr Edition, 1909, 283. Volume III was edited by Engels and published in 1894, eleven years after Marx's death. It has the great title, *The Process of Capitalist Production as a Whole*. Nudged by James Joyce's brand of wit, I think of the end word as *Hole* and then note that my little book has been about the Hole Story.

[11] Here you are: an axial sport's, Aristotle's, talk of the positive Anthropocene: "Since our purpose is to speak about matters to do with character, we must first inquire of what character is a branch. To speak concisely, then, it would seem to be a branch of nothing else than statecraft. For it is not possible to act at all in affairs of state unless one is of a certain kind, to wit, good. Now to be good is to possess the excellences. If therefore one is to act successfully in affairs of state, one must be of good character. The treatment of character then is, as it seems, a branch and starting point of statecraft. And as a whole it seems to me that the subject ought rightly to be called, not Ethics, but Politics." *The Complete Works of Aristotle*, edited

schools"? The solving of that problem, with a three-volume patience of someone like Marx, can be identified with the massive cultural change talked about skimpily in Part Three, with the road to an "Arrival in Cosmopolis" ending, by then, 20,000 years of the negative Anthropocene Age.[12]

Read now again that powerful paragraph at note 10. Have I brought you to a suspicion that the seed of the answer is there, neglected pointings of seventy-five years ago? Did Lonergan really leap to the discovery of economic science? Did Michael Faraday leap to the science of radiation?[13]

There is no point in my developing the parallel and the parallel in the story that is to come. What is important is our weaving round, vortex-powered, the Faraday-like jump to the equivalent in situation analysis of Maxwell, Einstein, Schrödinger, Feynman etc. My "Arriving in Cosmopolis" gives us seven millennia to sow the seed effectively. Do you think that too long? Well, do something about it!

But what?

Yes, what! What, energetically, about chapter two, and begin to annoy the community of professorial economics by asking them, "What about this: the two types of firm?" They will have apparently learned dodges, so you may have to what seriously and energetically about chapter three, about Joey, and credit, and rhythms, and the noting of talent and the talent of noting that the surge adds something extra, a surplus of promise and its moneyed measure, a surplus that is somehow loose and pure and that can be weaved forward, a pure surplus in the village and the globe. "This pure surplus income is quite an interesting thing," [14] but our culture is massively

---

by Jonathan Barnes (Princeton: Princeton University Press, 1984), vol. 2, 1868 (the first paragraph of the *Magna Moralia*).

[12] My article "Arriving in Cosmopolis" pessimistically points to the institution of Situation Room Analysis in the 10th millennium. I use here one of the estimates of the length of the Anthropocene age: having a start about 12 millennia ago. There are narrow estimates, e.g., a start with the industrial revolution. Sometimes I think we should include Lucy falling from the tree: was it a carelessness of the lady's *what*?

[13] Faraday's (1791–1867) law of induction grew into one of Maxwell's (1831–79) four equations that weave into present theory and its concrete problematic. What strange equations will dominate global economics? One might follow up this parallel as earlier I did that between studies of local water movements and of local economic movements. See note 7 on page 32 above.

[14] *For a New Political Economy*, 293. Likely written by Lonergan in 1943. It is repeated in the later text: *Macroeconomic Dynamics: An Essay in Circulation Analysis*, 146.

disinterested, dedicatedly disinterested. Certainly, when our culture, or the culture of the next millennium or so, rises out of its dedication to a Borg-cube stupidity and cupidity, there will emerge an effective global answer to the presidential questions of 1960 and to Marx's powerful questioning of the previous century. But the crisis question is here and now with you: do you now find pure surplus income interesting enough to get some initial grip on it, enough to annoy the economists, the journalists, the politicians? I recall again the book mentioned at the end of the Preface, Ron Suskind's sweep through *Wall Street, Washington, and the Education of a President*. The president was President Obama. The 500-page book bears witness to the truth of Lonergan's claim: "now it is true that our culture cannot be accused of mistaken ideas on pure surplus income as it has been defined in this essay; for on that precise topic it has no ideas whatever."[15] Will the same be true of our 2020 vision of, and in, Wall Street and Washington?

---

[15] *For a New Political Economy*, 297–98. (Note that, finally, and indeed in a final footnote, I have brought you towards being able to begin to read the key pages on the meaning of profit: *Ibid.*, 292–301.) A small business makes its owner an ordinary profit that the owner can consider as income for his or her standard of living: as basic income, in the way described. If that owner—let's think of Joey in chapter three, but now with an idea about innovation internal to the business—implements an idea that is, somehow, cost-saving, then, in the normal experience of such a move, there emerges a flow of extra income that, yes, could be self-cossetingly weaved into Joey's standard of living. Business people recognize this: they are "receiving an additional sum of income which is profit in their strong sense of the term." *Ibid.*, 293. That income is beyond what is needed for replacement and maintenance: these are already 'accounted for.' So, might we not handily call this income *pure surplus income*? Note that it is associated with some bright idea, be it about a new chemical of farm or pharma, or a new delivery route. And it is also associated with the meaning of *success*: for that particular meaning "it must be possible to derive from the circuits a rate of income that can be moved, without conflicting with circuit requirements, to the redistribution function." *Ibid.*, 294. Our dalliance with Joey was a shift from 'must' to fact, and we got some sense of "the fact that it is subject to cyclic variations in the long-term acceleration of the productive process." *Ibid.* From an analysis of an accumulation of such rhythmic facts (*ibid.*, 294–97): those pages give impossibly compact pointers to such an analysis, pointers that look back at the classifications and sophistications talked of in earlier pages there. The analysis is parallel to a swimming pool analysis of hydrodynamics, suitable for a first year university course. In reality, we face botched facts, yet we become poised to be able to understand such a statement as "at the root of the depression lies a misinterpretation of the significance of pure surplus income. In fact it is the monetary equivalent of the new fixed investment

of an expansion." *Ibid.*, 297. Think now back round about Joey's enterprise, a venture, "in the old days." "In the old days, when the entrepreneur was also owner and manager, pure surplus income coincided with what was termed profit. Today, with increasing specialization of function, pure surplus income is distributed in a variety of ways." *Ibid.*, 298: follow the text there. "Thus pure surplus income may be identified best of all by calling it net aggregate savings and viewing them as functionally as related to the rate of new fixed investment." *Ibid.* If you pause over this you find a tricky task of envisaging Joey's dealings with credit from the banker over the period of expansion. "Net aggregate savings vary with new fixed investment, and the complaint is that there exist, in the mentality of our culture, no ideas, and in the procedure of our economies, no mechanisms, directed to smoothly and equitably bringing about" (*ibid.*) the required normative rhythms, the **concomitances** I wrote of earlier. (31) And especially this is true of a cultural admission that at the end of an expansion, "net aggregate savings or pure surplus income have to be zero." *Ibid.*, 301. The island, and its various standards of living, are dynamically comfortable. But we need to move from the island to the globe—think of chapters seven and eight now—and of leaving the swimming pool for the ocean. Add, if you like, for we must do this, the envisagement of empirically strange impossible different levels and indeed, 'colors' of oceans: living-standards and needs vary, lag, leap ahead in different zones. The net aggregate savings weave into the problem of global credit: how do we rise to consider, e.g., local net aggregate savings as a global dividend (see note 24 on p. 112) in that global caring? We do so only under the pressure of an evolutionary whatting in layered situation-rooms of massive topological complexity. It is a vast task, and a topic of the remainder both of future undergraduate economics and of humanity's pilgrimage. The task involves, I would note in conclusion, the eventual disappearance of the idiot jugglings with money as a commodity that have developed in the past century: shall we say that it is a matter of people growing up luminously and self-luminosity to give credit where credit is due?

85148109R00091

Made in the USA
San Bernardino, CA
16 August 2018